Desirée Mays

OPERA UNVEILED

2013

THE SANTA FE OPERA

To order individual copies of *Opera Unveiled 1999 - 2013*
please send a check for $15 (postage included) to:
The Santa Fe Opera
PO Box 2408
Santa Fe, New Mexico 87504
Email: shop@santafeopera.org

Contents

La Donna del Lago
Gioacchino Rossini

9

The Grand Duchess of Gerolstein
Jacques Offenbach

23

Oscar
Theodore Morrison

35

La Traviata
Giuseppe Verdi

53

The Marriage of Figaro
Wolfgang Amadeus Mozart

67

La Donna del Lago

Gioacchino Rossini

Harp of the North! O minstrel Harp!
Must thine accents sleep?
Mid rustling leaves and fountain's murmuring,
Still must thy sweeter sounds their silence keep,
Nor bid a warrior smile, nor teach a maid to weep?

Thus Sir Walter Scott begins his tale, *The Lady of the Lake*, with an invocation to music. Songs, lays, laments, and choruses fill the verses of his romantic poem, making it a perfect piece for music and opera. The source of the story came from "the hint of an incident stemming from the frequent custom of James V, the King of Scotland, of walking through the kingdom in disguise." In this roaming, the historical king, born in 1513, learned the true condition of his subjects and took an interest in their welfare. From such snippets great literature and poetry is born.

Born in Edinburgh, Scott was in love with his native Scottish countryside for its natural beauty and ancient ruins; his first book was a collection of Scottish ballads. He is famous for the Waverley novels which include *Rob Roy*, *Ivanhoe*, and the *Bride of Lammermoor*, the story which inspired Donizetti. Scott has been called the inventor of the Romantic historical novel and was widely read in the 19th century becoming somewhat of a cult figure in Europe when *The Lady of the Lake* appeared in translation soon after its publication in 1810. Scott reported that he had spent much time as a young man in the Highlands, in "the land of lakes and glens, deep valleys, tall mountains, and brave men," and particularly in the region of Loch Katrine where *The Lady of the Lake* is set. "The action of this poem, which lay amongst scenes so beautiful, was a labor of love," he reported.

The men of the Highlands were Celts, driven north by the Romans. Their allegiance was first and foremost to their clan chiefs, and secondly to the King of Scotland. Territorial, fierce and brave, these fighters were constantly at war with the men of the Lowlands. The Lady of the Lake, inspired by Arthurian legends, is Ellen, daughter of the banished Douglas of Angus, a Highland Chieftain exiled from court by the king. Douglas sought and found refuge for his wife, daughter and supporters on a small island, called Ellen's Isle today, in the middle of Lake Katrine. Ellen has three suitors: Roderick, the fierce chief of a Highland clan who provides protection to Douglas; Malcolm Graeme, the warrior she loves; and James Fitz-James, (Uberto in the opera) the stranger who falls in love with Ellen. The stranger is, in reality, the King of Scotland, thus the enemy of the Douglas clan. The historical James V loved to hunt and this is where the story starts.

The overture is brief, the scene reveals an idyllic spot in the Scottish Highlands on the shore of Loch Katrine. It is dawn, shepherds and shepherdesses sing on their way to tend their flocks, hunters are heard in the distance accompanied by echoing solo horns, played in different parts of the theatre. Suddenly, a small boat appears on the lake steered by a young woman, Ellen, who sings a glorious aria in the early morning light: "O, mattutini albori!" (Oh, beautiful dawn). The lovely theme of her opening aria is heard throughout much of the opera. Joyce DiDonato, Santa Fe's Ellen, says of the role: "Rossini did his star a big favor by giving her such a perfect piece to warm up the voice at the start of this vocal marathon. The fluidity and simplicity of the music, I believe, shows us the purity of Elena as she begins her search for peace."

The king, in disguise as Uberto, has become separated from his fellow hunters on the shores of the lake. He blows his hunting horn to summon them, but there is no answering call, instead he sees movement on the lake as Ellen's small boat approaches. He stands in awe as he watches the Lady of the Lake come ashore:

> *The maiden paused, as if again,*
> *She thought to catch the distant strain.*
> *With head upraised and look intent,*
> *And eye and ear attentive bent,*
> *And locks flung back, and lips apart,*
> *Like monument of Grecian art,*
> *In listening mood she seemed to stand,*
> *The guardian Naiad of the strand*
> Lady of the Lake, Canto I, XVI

Ellen has heard the horn and thinks it is her father or Malcolm, the man she loves, returning to the island. She moors the little boat, sees the stranger and asks who he is. James tells her he is a hunter who is lost. Ellen, according to the laws of hospitality in the Highlands, invites him to return with her in her boat to her home. Uberto is overwhelmed with conflicting feelings of attraction for this "sylvan goddess" who has appeared like a vision, and the potential danger of being discovered by his enemies.

He chooses to accompany Ellen to the island where she promises him shelter, a meal and a bed for the night. Uberto, looking around the simple dwelling, recognizes the arms of a noble house and learns that Ellen's father is Douglas of Angus. Uberto is surprised and realizes at once the danger if he is recognized.

Ellen's friends, led by Albina, arrive and sing her praises comparing her to a heroine of Celtic myth: "The damsel of Inibaca once, long ago, caused the heart of Tremmor to melt with boundless passion." They tell that she has, in similar fashion, melted the heart of Roderick, their Highland protector. Ellen sighs for she loves Malcolm, not Roderick, and Uberto sighs for he is falling for Ellen and is dismayed to learn he has a rival in Roderick. Uberto asks if she is betrothed and she intimates she loves another, whom Uberto, misunderstanding, hopes is himself. And yet, he senses: "Her fleeting glances tell me otherwise," while she sings to herself "In just one flash all happiness was denied me." Uberto tells her he must leave and he is escorted to the shore by the women.

On a bare stage, Malcolm Graeme, Ellen's beloved, (who is sung by a mezzo-soprano), now appears and expresses his love for Ellen in his entrance aria. He wonders if she is still faithful. When he leaves, Douglas, Ellen's father, arrives and informs Ellen that he has decided that she is to be wed to the brave hero, Roderick. Ellen, seeking time, tells her father this is no time for talk of betrothals when they are at war. Her father, incensed at her delaying tactics, orders her to obey. Malcolm, overhearing this, begins to realize Ellen still loves him and, when the coast is clear, they run to one another's arms to re-affirm their love in a tender duet.

Trumpets announce the arrival of Roderick who is greeted by his clansmen in a rousing chorus. He takes center stage and vows to lead his men to victory. Following his rallying cry to his men, there is a complete change of character in Roderick as he now sings tenderly of his longing for Ellen. His supporters assure him Love will grant his wish. Douglas approaches Roderick and embraces him as Roderick asks about Ellen, why is she not there to greet him? Ellen appears, but pays little attention to her enthusiastic suitor. This all leads into a lively trio between the angry Douglas, the confused Roderick and the distraught Ellen. In the course of the trio, Douglas comes to realize that his daughter loves Malcolm: "Anger and vexation tear my breast apart." Ellen despairs: "Dear God, release me from this ordeal," while Roderick guesses something is seriously wrong: "Dark suspicions rankle in me. Now I understand and my fury rises!"

But for the moment, marriage negotiations and romance must wait as the clans prepare for war against the king and his forces. Malcolm offers his sword to Roderick vowing to fight, with his men, under Roderick's leadership. The finale that ends Act I, the famous war hymn "Già un raggio forier" (Behold! Already a prophetic light) is a magnificent ensemble piece, a number that was popular with Italian patriots over the next 50 years in their struggle for unity and independence. Roderick invites the Bards to "sing the songs that will inspire our men and spur them on." The Bards sing the great chorus accompanied by harps, violas and pizzicato cellos. This chorus is steeped in many traditions: in the Scott poem it is the ritual of the Fiery Cross in which a cross of wood is made, dipped in the blood of a sacrificial animal, set alight and then carried from glen to glen calling the men of the hills to gather, to meet and fight at the side of their Chieftain. Those who do not heed the call of the Fiery Cross suffer certain death.

Roderick steps forward and, in another ancient Scottish tradition, strikes the great shield which reportedly once belonged to the mythic leader Tremmor. The warriors follow his example beating their swords on their shields. In the opera, a meteor flashes across the sky before the assembled clans, and is described by the Bards: "Behold! Already a prophetic light of rare splendor shows the way to glory and honor." Roderick interprets the meteor as "an unmistakable omen of resounding victory." Now, in addition to the orchestra, Rossini concludes the finale with an onstage *banda* of wind and brass with clarinets, trumpets and trombones for a rousing send-off to war and the act ends with the clans marching off to battle as Ellen and the women pray for victory.

Act II begins, like Act I, with the king once more in disguise as Uberto. He has come to seek Ellen: "I've lost my reason! Ellen, let me have but one glimpse of you." He hides as Ellen appears with Serano, her father's retainer. She is concerned because her father has not returned from the fighting and Serano leaves to find him. Ellen is startled when Uberto appears and wonders why he has returned. He tells her of his love for her; she is taken aback, she does not return his love but does not want him to suffer on her behalf. Once again, she and Uberto sing at cross purposes. Finally Uberto understands she loves another and agrees to leave, but before doing so he gives her a ring "as a pledge of my fidelity. If ever adversity should befall you, go to the king and he will pardon you." They sing of their mutual unhappiness just as Roderick, overhearing them, arrives and assumes the stranger is Ellen's lover. The men argue fiercely and draw their weapons. Roderick calls his followers who rush to attack Uberto as Ellen runs between them and begs for peace.

Later, Malcolm, having missed all this action, comes looking for Ellen but she is nowhere to be found. He tells Albina that Roderick is duelling some way off with an unknown opponent. Serano reports that Douglas, realizing defeat was imminent, has gone to the king to give himself up and ask for mercy for his clansmen. Ellen has gone in pursuit of her father. Roderick's warriors announce that their leader has been killed in the duel; the stranger and the King of Scotland, whom they do not know are one and the same, has won.

In the final scenes calm prevails as the location changes to the royal apartments of Stirling Castle. Ellen arrives and uses the ring the stranger gave her to see the king. Uberto sings offstage (in a technique widely used later by Verdi) of his longing for Ellen. She meets him and reminds him of his promise. Will he take her to the king? "Uberto" guides her to a great door and opens it revealing the magnificent throne room. The people bow at Uberto's entrance and slowly Ellen realizes the truth: Uberto is the King. "Could you be?" she gasps, "Oh God, dispel my doubts." She falls at his feet and he raises her up. "What is it you desire?" She says her father's name and Douglas is brought in. The king pardons him then orders that Malcolm be brought in. James tells Malcolm he warrants no pity, but then, taking a gold chain off his own neck he places it on Malcolm. The king joins the hands of the lovers as Ellen bursts into an aria of brilliant coloratura, "Tanti affetti in tal momento" (So many emotions well up in my heart, I cannot express my thankfulness) as the opera ends, as it must, with general rejoicing. Joyce DiDonato describes this final aria: "Elena is overcome with joy and the vocal fireworks that paint this elation serve as an incredible expression of unrepressed abandon."

Gioacchino Rossini was jet-setting (or the 19th-century equivalent) around Italy at the time of the composition of *La donna del lago*. The year was 1819, a year that started with the success of his revised *Mosè in Egitto* in Naples, followed by the failure of the premiere of *Ermione* (an opera Rossini said "would not see the light of day until after my death" – he was right). Then a quick trip to Venice where he was feted for *Eduardo e Cristina*. This was followed by a journey to his home town, Pesaro, where he expected to be welcomed but ran into trouble with a jealous enemy, Bergami, who virtually ran Rossini out of town. Rossini never visited his hometown again. Once back in Naples, he and his librettist, Andrea Leone Tottola, got to work on *La donna del lago* – and this was only June.

Rossini had been given a copy of the Scott narrative poem in French and was immediately drawn to the Scottish tale which was quite a departure from his usual style and choice of topic. The *melodramma* in two acts was composed in a very short time and under tremendous pressure, but it set the vogue for operas based on Walter Scott's stories and was an enormous success at its premiere at the Teatro San Carlo in Naples on October 21. Then Rossini was off to Milan for his next new opera which opened at La Scala on the day after Christmas. This whirlwind composer was at his creative peak – and only 28 years old. Rossini experienced one success after another in Naples with the best singers and orchestra in the operatic world.

The orchestration conjures up almost stereophonic effects as one hears six solo horns calling back and forth to one another during the hunt, at once setting the mood and the color of the work. *La donna del lago* was a venture that led Rossini into uncharted musical territory for, in this opera, he did not follow the typical *opera seria* style with pauses in the action for extended arias interspersed with explanatory recitatives. Rossini's score points the way to music drama while retaining some entrance arias for his principals. There is a novel contrast in the duets between Ellen and Uberto who sing together but at cross purposes, and the Ellen/Malcolm duets which are firmly bound in a warm, vocal embrace. The many tender and sweet moments of delicacy in this opera make the score almost chamber-like, while the rousing choruses are vintage Rossini.

The great Act II trio "Alla ragion deh reida"(Calm yourself, be reasonable) begins as a duet between Ellen and Uberto then ratchets up to a series of high Cs from the two tenors, Uberto and Roderick, as they vie for supremacy in high flying vocal fireworks until Uberto presumably wins with a high D. Joyce DiDonato describes this as an "Olympian trio and a battle for the high Cs; Rossini at his athletic best." This is all capped, brilliantly, by the entrance of the chorus in full voice to support Roderick.

There is a marked sense of locale in this opera, something else that was new for Rossini, with the setting in the misty hills and lakes of Scotland and, the most inspired moment of all, Ellen's mystical appearance as the Lady of the Lake rippling her way across Loch Katrine at the start. In addition, the use of harp and horns helps conjure up ancient Celtic lands and customs.

Though Scott's *Lady of the Lake* is the primary source for the opera, the librettist Tottola was also intrigued by the epic Celtic tales of Ossian. These tales were published as a series of poems in 1760 by James Macpherson, a man who claimed to have gathered together fragments of ancient, epic poems, translated and published them. The poems, taken from ancient Irish mythology, tell of the exploits of Finn McCool, as told by Oisin, his son and the narrator of the tales. Critics insisted the poems were not original but were written by Macpherson himself. The Irish insisted Macpherson had hijacked their myth. Samuel Johnson called Macpherson a liar and a fraud. Johnson pointed out that the ancient language had not been written down at the time of the myths, but Macpherson disagreed and insisted his collection was drawn from original sources. The battle about authenticity raged on amongst European literati until the mid-1950s (for 200 years!) when a compromise was reached: some of the ballads probably came from original sources but Macpherson introduced many of his own. Regardless, the poems achieved phenomenal success: Napoleon and Thomas Jefferson loved them; Goethe included them in *The Sorrows of Young Werther* and the young Walter Scott was much influenced by them. Schubert composed songs set to Ossian poems, Mendelssohn composed his *Fingal's Cave* overture under their influence.

Macpherson strove to recreate the poetic meter of the bards of old in a 'measured prose.' Rossini and Tottola in turn strove to interweave a sense of these very rhythms into the score and libretto. The result, for Rossini, was a score that, unlike his earlier works, was through-composed in a story-telling manner.

Here is an example of the comparable styles of Scott's poetry, which was influenced by the Ossian cycle, and the libretto of Tottola at the point where Uberto sings of his longing for Ellen:

Walter Scott:	Tottola:
No more at dawning morn I rise	*Ah, dawn! Will you always rise*
And sun myself in Ellen's eyes	*to taunt me with visions of Ellen?*
Drive the fleet deer the forest through	*reminding me of her*
And homeward wend with evening dew	*and thereby ravishing me?*
While fled the eve on wings of glee	*Is that all you can offer,*
That life is lost to love and me!	*Barbarous dawn!*
Canto VI, XXIV	Uberto's aria: "Aurora! Ah sorgerai"

Stefano Castelvecchi, in his paper, "Walter Scott, Rossini et la Couleur Ossianique" argues for the presence of Ossian references in the libretto and for the influence of the older poetic meter on the structure, both of which lend the opera a sense of mystery with connections to a mythological past. Rossini's *La donna del lago* was immensely popular all over Europe following the premiere in 1819. It played in London in the 1820s and in New York in the early 1830s, then it dropped out of the repertoire for over 100 years only returning in 1969 with a young Kiri te Kanawa singing Elena. In 1992, it returned to its rightful place in the repertoire with performances at La Scala during Rossini's bi-centennial under the baton of Riccardo Muti. Part of the problem of producing this opera is that it cannot be done without outstanding leading singers. In addition to the soprano, Elena, there are two tenors, Uberto and Roderick, and a mezzo-soprano who sings the role of Malcolm in the tradition of Rossini's time when the role of a younger man was generally sung by a woman. Elena's father, Douglas, is a bass.

Joyce DiDonato hails from Kansas and is one of the most beloved singers in the world today. Attributed as the singer who has "set a new gold standard for Rossini," she has specialized in the challenging roles of Rossini's repertoire. Her *La Cenerentola* and Rosina in *The Barber of Seville* are now legendary roles, especially her Rosina which she sang famously at Covent Garden in a wheelchair with her leg (broken in an on-stage fall) in a pink cast. She said it worked since Rosina lives her life in a cage, which is just how DiDonato felt singing from a wheelchair.

She made her debut appearance as Elena in *La donna del lago* at Switzerland's Grand Théâtre de Genève in May, 2010 and sang the role again a month later, in a completely new production at La Scala opposite Juan Diego Florez in June! The Telegraph raved about her performance at London's Wigmore Hall: " 'Tanti affetti' was a knockout, from the heart-stopping cadenza to the dreamy cavatina and sparkling fireworks in the triumphant cabaletta that left the entire audience with a silly smile on its collective face."

DiDonato described her feelings when taking curtain calls for her Elena at La Scala in 2011 on the anniversary of her father's death: "I dedicated the show to him. Singing the final aria with the opening words 'Fra il padre, e fra l'amante o qual beato istante." (My father, my beloved! This moment is blessed!) carried a profound meaning for me that night, and in taking the final curtain call, my only thought was that I hoped he had heard it. I believe very much in the power of music to connect all of us in unimaginable ways, as well as in its power to help us understand that which is illusionary. I'm more grateful than I can say for the chance to explore this world in the greatest theaters in the world."

The Santa Fe production will be directed by Paul Curran, a favorite director in Santa Fe *(La Bohème, Billy Budd, Peter Grimes, Albert Herring)*; Lawrence Brownlee, one of the most acclaimed *bel canto* tenors of our time, sings Uberto/the king; and mezzo-soprano Marianna Pizzolato sings Malcolm. The set, by Kevin Knight, will show the stony ground of the Highlands, Elena will arrive on a little sailboat and the costumes will be colorful kilts and sashes – a Romantic look overall, as Walter Scott, and Rossini, intended.

So, *La donna del lago* has all the ingredients for a great night at the opera, it even has a happy, over-the-top romantic ending, one that Sir Walter Scott brings to a close with a farewell to the Harp of the North:

Receding now the dying numbers ring
A wandering witch note of the distant spell -
And now 'tis silent all - Enchantress, fare thee well!

♪

Characters

Elena (Ellen)	Soprano
Malcolm Graeme	Mezzo-soprano
Uberto (King James V)	Tenor
Rodrigo di Dhu (Roderick)	Tenor
Douglas d'Angus	Bass

Bibliography

Castelvecchi, Stefano, "Walter Scott, Rossini et a Couleur Ossianique." Bollettino del Centro Rossiano studi, 1993.

Gossett, Philip. "La donna del lago and the revival of the Rossini opera seria." CD: CBS Records, M2K39311, Maurizio Pollini, conductor.

Osborne, Richard, *Rossini*. Oxford University Press, 2007.

Scott, Walter, *The Lady of the Lake*. Fredonia Books, The Netherlands, 2001.

Jacques Offenbach by Hippolyte Mailly

The Grand Duchess of Gerolstein

Jacques Offenbach

The *Grand Duchess of Gerolstein* is a comic romp of waltzes, *galops*, military marches and rousing music set, in Santa Fe's production, in a Military Academy in the United States with the outrageous, fictitious Duchess as patroness of the establishment. This intentionally satirical piece about military preparedness, war games and political manoeuverings was an immediate success for its composer, Jacques Offenbach, and his leading lady, Hortense Schneider, when it first appeared at the tiny Théâtre Variétés in Paris in 1867. The Duchess manages an entire army promoting men up and down the official ranks while falling in and out of love with the nearest good-looking man at a moment's notice. That is pretty much the plot.

Top military men, politicians and the royalty of Europe flocked to see this amusing parody of themselves; satire in a humorous vein is always an antidote to the realities of everyday life. People need to laugh though, in this case, history was repeating itself for, just as French nobility laughed at the antics of Figaro and his creator Beaumarchais and then lost their heads in the French Revolution, so too in 1867, high society laughed, with both Bismarck and Napoleon III in the audience, shortly before their entire way of life in the Second Empire came tumbling down during the Franco-Prussian War of 1870. The Champs-Élysée was the center of this hedonistic, glamorous and scandalous world with two tiny theatres, the Bouffes-Parisiens and the Variétés, and with Jacques Offenbach, nicknamed Mozart of the Boulevards, as the superstar who provided endless exciting evenings of theatre for the rich and famous. Midway through his astonishing career, *The Grand Duchess of Gerolstein*, his 29th opera, was possibly his greatest success.

Even Tsar Alexander II checked out the opéra bouffe everyone was talking about in part to make sure there was no untoward criticism of Russia, concerned because he heard the Duchess parodied his autocratic ancestor, Catherine the Great. However, the lively music of Offenbach and the witticisms of the cast reassured him and he applauded the work. Visitors who came to Paris ostensibly for the World Exhibition flocked to the Variétés for the hottest show in town, tickets in the tiny theatre were at a premium. But beneath the frivolity Offenbach and his librettists seriously addressed the timeless issues of the headiness of power, favoritism, and the misuse of the army and war to further personal ambition. Fritz, the apparently clueless soldier at the center of the plot, may not be aware of what is going on but some members of Offenbach's audience understood the deeper implications of the plot.

How did Jacques Offenbach get away with all this? Offenbach, son of a German cantor, struggled mightily at the start of his career. He studied music at the Paris Conservatoire in his early teens then joined the orchestra of the Opéra-Comique as a cellist, a job that introduced him to the world of operetta on a nightly basis; it was here, in the dark pit of the Opéra-Comique that Offenbach learned his craft and found his calling. He wrote background music for plays at the Comédie Française conducting from the pit in full evening dress, but what he really wanted was to compose operas. He applied repeatedly to the Opéra-Comique with new operas in hand, but was always rejected. Frustrated and disappointed, Offenbach finally decided, with the backing of influential friends, to buy and renovate a small, abandoned theatre with space for only 16 musicians in the cramped pit, and present his works there. He called his theatre, which opened in 1855, the Bouffes-Parisiens and from there Offenbach's irresistibly catchy melodies radiated out into the streets of Paris. He laced his popular music with the saucy satire that became his trademark. Never vicious, his satire was always presented in a spirit of fun. Contemporary composers, Wagner, Meyerbeer, the court, the establishment – all came under his satirical eye, and all laughed with Offenbach. Paris was happy to laugh at herself in those days, and Offenbach provided the means.

Opéra bouffe, the operatic style for which Offenbach was so famous, took its very name from his theatre. The style was developed by him in reaction to the more formalized *opéra-comique*. Opéra bouffe is comic opera in which witty and sophisticated spoken dialogue is combined with light, sparkling music. The golden age of both opéra bouffe and operetta (*opérette* in French, *opera buffa* in Italian) with their romantic tales and happy endings, saw its heyday in the second half of the 19th century, and came to an abrupt end with the Franco-Prussian war. Following the war, opéra bouffe fell out of favor as times and tastes changed. In England and America the trend Offenbach started picked up and came to be known as musical comedy which made its debut in those countries as the next step in the evolution of light opera.

Offenbach was fortunate to team up with Ludovic

Halévy and Henri Meilhac, outstanding librettists who wrote witty and sophisticated books satirizing the Paris of Napoleon III. (Years later, Halévy and Meilhac would write the libretto for Bizet's *Carmen*.) In addition to finding the best librettists, Offenbach had a gift for spotting new, young, and gifted singers. His discovery of the beautiful and talented singer-comédienne, Hortense Schneider, completed the team which was to work together for many years on many productions.

Schneider made her debut at the Bouffes-Parisiens at age 22, a month after the theatre opened, and audiences and critics raved about her from the start. Thanks to Offenbach, she became the reigning sex symbol of Paris overnight, and threw herself with equal abandon into the life of the theatre and numerous love affairs. Her list of noble, wealthy lovers grew quickly, causing a malicious rival to name her "Passage des Princes." Even the influential Duc de Morny loved her in a relationship that lasted for years. She was known for her temper and tantrums, but always came through in performance. The role of the Duchess was composed for Hortense Schneider.

A story is told of Schneider at the time of the World Exhibition which coincided with *The Grand Duchess of Gerolstein's* opening. She arrived in a carriage to drive around the Exhibition and was told that only royalty were allowed this privilege. She drew herself up and announced grandly: "But I am the Duchess of Gerolstein," at which the startled gatekeepers at once bowed low and let her pass.

Offenbach was at the peak of his career when *The Grand Duchess* premiered in April 1867; five of his pieces were playing simultaneously in Paris that spring. The first act went well with a critic reporting: "It is delightful, incredibly imaginative, sparkling with gaiety, the most comical indictment of military glory imaginable, with its plumes, its braid and all the rest of its trappings." But there were problems from the second act on, and the piece was far too long. Undaunted, Offenbach made the necessary changes, cutting and refining the work so that it quickly became a success playing to sold-out houses. The censors, however, were far from happy at Offenbach's depiction of imperial power. In spite of the fact the show was set in an imaginary 18th-century duchy with a leading lady titled Gerolstein, nobody was fooled; this satire was about contemporary France. Henri Meihac and Ludovic Halévy, Offenbach's librettists, fought an ongoing battle to appease the censors who disapproved of the Duchess, her military attire and the risqué situations in which she embroils herself. A Duchess could not be seen simultaneously pursuing a lowly soldier and a baron who happened to be her fiancé's emissary. The singers had to agree to stay with the script with no ad-libbing or topical asides, techniques that had really contributed to Offenbach's earlier successes, *La Belle Hélène* and *La Vie Parisienne*. A journalist described *The Grand Duchess* as: "This adorable parody of everything to do with war and old-style politics, with outrageous fun poked at those little German courts where etiquette held sway as long as some faded little princeling ruled there." Halévy wrote in his diary at the time: "This time it's war we are laughing at, and war is at our gates." The Franco-Prussian war did indeed put an effective end to *The Grand Duchess*. Anti-militarism was no longer seen as comic when the country faced an all-too-real war, the opera was banned.

The opera requires seven principals, including an outstanding soprano to sing and play the Duchess, with a number of smaller roles and a large chorus. Operetta, opéra bouffe or, for that matter, musical comedy, is made up of a series of musical numbers interspersed with dialogue. In order for English-speaking audiences to understand the dialogue, and to "get" the colloquial references, many opera companies today, including The Santa Fe Opera, present the musical numbers in the original language and the dialogue in English. For comic dialogue to work the audience must be able to understand the words.

Director Lee Blakeley has decided to set the Santa Fe production in the Gerolstein Military Academy on this side of the Atlantic. The period is the turn of the 20th century without the Franco-Prussian war looming over the piece, though the satire of politics and the military still rings true. Blakeley feels this comic piece should be set in a time and place with which the audience can identify. He prepared the show in close collaboration with its star, Susan Graham, for this, "make no mistake about it, is Susan's show," he says. The Duchess is often played as an older woman, almost as a character role, but Blakeley felt that given "our vibrant, young and sexy" star the production should be built around her as a lively, somewhat spoiled and tyrannical Duchess who seeks love in all the wrong places.

The lively opening is set in the Gerolstein Military Academy revealing happy soldiers preparing for war games that look more like track and field events as they "waltz and whirl" around the stage with their girlfriends. Apparently the soldiers are to go to war with an unidentified opponent. Though this doesn't make any sense, they are soldiers and are ready for whatever comes at a moment's notice. Fritz, an inconsequential soldier, stands to one side watching the goings-on. He catches the eye of a young woman, Wanda, who flirts with him. General Boum, who also has an eye for Wanda, bombastically enters and orders the women out of the camp in one of the hit songs of the show: "Through valleys I ride straight ahead; I wipe out whole battalions with a pif, paf, pouf and a tara papa poum." The chorus dutifully joins in the merriment: "Vive le General Boum!"

Boum dresses down Fritz and separates him from Wanda. Fritz is ordered to stand on guard and not speak to anyone which is fine until Wanda reappears, embroils him in a duet which ends with a kiss and another, and another.

Baron Puck and the General explain that the games have been devised as an amusement for their patron, the Duchess, who is bored. Her Highness, the Grand Duchess, is announced and makes her great entrance on the military parade ground. She has come to review her regiment, award prizes and inspect her cadets: "How I love soldiers with their flattering uniforms, their masterful air and soldiers' ways," she sings. In a truly farcical style, the men hang on her every word. Now the dialogue takes over as the Duchess surveys her troops and spots a good-looking soldier who is not singing her praises. He is brought forward and she asks his name and about his battles and wounds. "Zero battles, zero wounds," Fritz replies. Splendid, she says and promotes him to corporal, then sergeant and captain in quick succession. Boum and Puck are appalled, Fritz is confused, but happily so.

Boum and Baron Puck, fellow-conspirators who are eager to hang onto power, talk about how they are concerned about the Duchess who is "glum, anxious and peevish." They decide to liven things up by declaring war on some unknown enemy. They have also found a husband for their Duchess, one Prince Paul, whom they hope to control, but she wants nothing to do with Prince Paul for the moment, not when she has just set her sights on Fritz.

Then it is time for the Regimental Song and there is general rejoicing when the Duchess offers to lead the song herself. This parody of a military song filled with taran tatas and rata-plans rouses everyone, including the audience, to fever pitch. The soldiers march off as Prince Paul makes his grand entrance in his bridegroom's outfit hoping to attract the Duchess who keeps putting him off. She hasn't time for him today, she would much rather see Fritz in his new uniform. The Prince is angry because the local paper makes a laughing stock of him in the gossip columns. The Duchess joins him in a funny duet in which the media are parodied for misrepresenting the facts in scandalous reporting. (Some things don't change.) The Duchess is amused, dismisses the sputtering Prince, and calls a war council with her advisors, Boum and Puck together with Fritz. They discuss the battle plan which is of course, ridiculous. Fritz says the plan is silly and suggests one of his own; the Duchess is delighted and promotes him to General to the fury of the rest. In an memorable ensemble piece, the Duchess bequeathes her late father's very own sabre to Fritz and the whole scene wraps up in the famous Sabre chorus. Fritz, at last finding a moment to himself, bids farewell to Wanda and promises he won't forget her. However, when the Duchess overhears their conversation, she has an instant attack of jealous nerves. Paul, Boum and Puck conspire to pool their resources to outwit this upstart soldier. The sabre is brought forward, the Duchess ceremoniously hands it to Fritz who promises to return victorious from the war as the act ends with a lively march to send the departing soldiers on their way.

In Act II a few days later, the war is over and the soldiers are returning victorious, of course. The Grand Duchess has been keeping track of their progress from a makeshift war cabinet set up in the Academy's ballroom. Her ladies read letters from their lovers sent to them from The Front in the amusing rhyming couplets (in French) that fill the libretto.

Boum, Puck and Paul, enraged by General Fritz's success, agree on a plan to get rid of him; this is where full blown melodrama kicks in. It turns out there is a bedroom in the palace that has a portrait of one of the Duchess's ancestors and behind it is a secret passage to the Duchess's room. In the past, a lover of an earlier Duchess was visited via the passage, not by the Duchess, but by assassins who killed him. Boum, Puck and Paul plan to re-enact this scenario with General Fritz. Well pleased with themselves, the three men melodramatically check out the secret buttons on the portrait. At the sound of a cannon everyone assembles to welcome home the jubilant General Fritz and his troops. The Duchess has Fritz give a blow by blow account of the battle which he does at length in his big aria. Victory was won by getting the enemy drunk. The Duchess announces a Victory Ball that night. Left alone with Fritz, she flirts with him and all but tells him she loves him. Fritz, either blind to her advances or pretending to be, tells her he hopes she will sign the wedding contract for him to marry Wanda at the Ball. The scorned, fickle Duchess saves what face she can and goes straight to the assassination trio and offers to join their plot to kill Fritz that very night.

The Ball begins; a notary, a wedding cake, Fritz and Wanda arrive. The Duchess, torn between her decision to kill Fritz, her attraction to him, and her anger at his loving someone else, is unsure how to proceed. Under pressure from Fritz, she signs the wedding contract before striking up the band for a rousing rendition of her grandmother's carillon song, another show-stopper. Fritz does not know that starting the carillon is the cue to the assassins for the plot to go ahead. The carillon is a slightly racy dance but the crowd enters into its spirit and general high-energy mayhem results. One should note here that Offenbach was the composer who made the can-can a nearly respectable dance by including it originally in his *galop infernal* in *Orpheus in the Underworld*. There are many such can-can or *galop* moments in *The Grand Duchess*.

The final act opens with a moment, at last, of introspection on the part of the Duchess. She sings a Meditation wondering how she could love a poor soldier one moment and then, when rejected, be complicit in his murder the next. She has serious second thoughts. Her co-conspirators arrive and, in a hilarious scene, sharpen their knives for their attack on the innocent, unarmed Fritz. They are joined by Baron Grog, the emissary for Prince Paul. On meeting the Baron, the Duchess now decides that he is the man of the moment for her. The wily Baron suggests she marry Prince Paul (his objective) then he will be able to stay nearby. The Duchess falls for this, cancels the assassination (it wouldn't do to have an assassination on her wedding day), and gives orders that preparations for her wedding to Prince Paul begin at once. Boum complains to the Duchess that he cannot now have revenge on Fritz and she tells him: "Have your revenge, but no killing."

The newly married couple, Fritz and Wanda, appear escorted by a wedding group to see them tucked in for the night – a good night, they insist. Just as the young couple are left alone and settling in, reveille is heard and Fritz starts up, "I must speak to them." He leaves Wanda to accept the greetings of his troops as the chorus enthusiastically sings "Vive le General!" Interruptions keep happening until Boum appears and informs General Fritz that the enemy has made a counter attack. Fritz doesn't want to leave but eventually takes off on a horse provided by General Boum.

Back at the camp everyone gathers to celebrate the marriage of the Duchess to Prince Paul. The Duchess sings a somewhat irrelevant ballad about a drunken ancestor and everyone indulges her. She suddenly remembers Fritz and asks what has become of him and Boum reveals his nasty plot of revenge. Fritz was saddled up on the horse that had taken Boum to his mistress's house for years, but her husband found out and now Boum is not welcome there –

but his horse doesn't know this and took Fritz directly to the lady's house where her husband gave him a royal beating. A disheveled and dirty, limping General Fritz appears, the Duchess's famous sabre twisted like a corkscrew in his hand, and tells his story. He is promptly demoted back down the ranks to where he started. By now Fritz has had enough and resigns from the army. The Duchess accepts his General's plume and turns to hand it to Grog, her new favorite, but Grog informs her his work is done and he is off back home to his wife and children. Stymied once more, the Duchess orders him out of her palace and turns to the Prince whom she now decides to love, saying: "When one cannot have what one loves, one must love what one has." Everyone ends up happy, the Duchess and the Prince, Fritz and Wanda, General Boum, Barons Puck and Grog as together they sing: "It's perfectly proper, that's how the play ends."

Sadly, the ending was not so happy for Jacques Offenbach. Following success after success in these heady years, 1870 came and with it the war between his beloved France and the land of his birth, Germany, and the tide turned for both France and Offenbach. The man, who was more French than the French themselves, found himself labeled "a Prussian at heart." By 1873 fickle audiences, tired of social satire, forgot how he had made them laugh, and turned to other composers for amusement. Offenbach and his family retreated to their home by the sea at Etretat. Offenbach composed many more operettas, but without the same success; he was soon bankrupt. He toured America where he was well received, but he missed his family and France. On his return home and in declining health, he worked on his final opera, the great *Les Contes d'Hoffmann* (The Tales of Hoffmann). This final opera was, at last, his entrée into the world of grand opera. In spite of his extraordinary success in the world of opéra bouffe,

Offenbach always wanted to be held in the esteem shown to Mozart and Rossini. He yearned to compose a work of art, a full-length grand opera. The opera was virtually complete and in rehearsal at the Opéra-Comique when Offenbach died. The premiere, which took place in February 1881, was a success. In the end, Offenbach was able to challenge the critics who had patronized him as a composer of mere opéra bouffe with his great final work, *Les Contes d'Hoffmann*, a work that is played worldwide today.

The Santa Fe cast of *The Grand Duchess* stars the magnificent Susan Graham, her Fritz is Paul Appleby, winner of numerous opera awards. The show is directed by Lee Blakeley and conducted by Emmanuele Villaume.

♪

Characters

The Grand Duchess	Soprano or mezzo
Fritz	Tenor
Wanda	Soprano
General Boum	Baritone
Baron Puck	Bass
Prince Paul	Tenor
Baron Grog	Bass

Bibliography

Grammond, Peter. *Offenbach: His Life and Times*. Midas Books, Kent, England, 1980.

Sadie, Stanley, ed., *The Grove Dictionary of Opera*. Macmillan Reference Ltd., London, 1998.

Yon, Jean-Claude, *La Grande-Duchesse de Gerolstéin: a political piece*. CD Offenbach. *La Grande-Duchesse de Gerolstein*. EMI Records/Virgin Classics, CD 7243 5 45734 22, 2005.

Oscar

Theodore Morrison and John Cox

O scar Fingal O'Flahertie Wills Wilde was Irish, born in Dublin in 1854 and educated first at Trinity College and then Oxford University in England. He, along with fellow compatriot, George Bernard Shaw, was proud of being Irish. Shaw commented on Oscar's kindness remembering how, when he was ill and in pain, Oscar came to see him once: "A visit from Oscar was like taking an anaesthetic because listening to his enchanted words you forgot everything else."

Oscar had colorful parents, Dr. William Wilde and Lady Jane "Speranza" Wilde. She was a writer, a poet and a fierce patriot who fought, with her pen, for the Nationalist Cause in Ireland. An intensely alive woman, she once said of herself: "I should like to rage through life – this orthodox creeping is too tame for me." She dressed outrageously, a characteristic she passed on to her son. In 1851, she met and married William Wilde, a brilliant eye and ear doctor and a man who shared her love of the history and myths of Ireland.

Given this background, Oscar and his brother, Willie,

were given the best education. In those days study of the Classics focused on Greek, Latin, Divinity, Literature and Poetry, Philosophy and Aesthetics, the study of nature and the expression of beauty. Oscar graduated with high honors, winning the prestigious Newdigate Prize when he left Oxford at the age of 23. He was a debonair and popular figure, known for his high spirits, generosity and sparkling conversation. He was also a flamboyant dresser who stated: "One should either be a work of art, or wear a work of art," along with "The only way to atone for occasionally being a little over-dressed is by being always, absolutely over-educated."

Oscar was drawn to the conflicting philosophies of two of his professors at Oxford: John Ruskin, who believed artists could "display their morality by fidelity to nature and by eschewing self-indulgence," and Walter Pater, who proposed living every moment to the full seeking "not the fruit of experience, but experience itself." Oscar ultimately chose the latter, to live in the manner of the ancient Greeks with their love of nature and beauty, art, and sculptures of Greek youth. Attracted to the Pre-Raphaelite movement in England at the time, his ambiguous sexuality and general contempt for conventional morality began to be apparent. He become a self-styled aesthete, a lover of beauty and art for its own sake, saying "Life imitates Art far more than Art imitates Life."

During his Oxford years Oscar had a close friendship, for a time, with a young Irish woman of good family and marriageable age, but he was already drawn to homosexuality, talked much about this taboo subject amongst his friends and began to have intimate relation-ships, mostly with college and literary associates.

When he graduated and arrived in London he did not have the inheritance that he might have expected for Sir William had died leaving his wife and two sons in debt.

The great Irish homes were sold and Lady Wilde moved to London, hosting brilliant salons where the intelligentsia met and talked. Always eccentric, mother and son entertained regally and brilliantly, throwing parties at which Oscar was always the center of attention. As a wit and fascinating conversationalist, he invented the art of being a celebrity. In those heady days, when still in his 20s, the Prince of Wales, a frequent guest at the salons, commented: "Not to know Oscar Wilde was not to be known." Oscar was drawn to the theatre in these years, thinking about writing for the stage. He adored actresses. When Sarah Bernhardt arrived in England for the first time, Oscar met her at the port and threw an armful of lilies at her feet. Later, much later, when he was in prison, she would play his *Salomé* at the premiere performances in Paris.

Oscar described his youthful philosophy of life in his early published poems. In *Hélas* (1881), he writes of how he longs:

> *To drift with every passion till my soul*
> *Is a stringed lute upon which all winds can play*
> *Is it for this I have given away*
> *Mine ancient wisdom and austere control?*

In 1882, Oscar undertook a lecture tour of America. His topics were: "The Beautiful as seen in everyday Life" and "The English Renaissance." This extensive, year-long tour made Oscar a household name on both sides of the Atlantic. He was feted, wined and dined wherever he went as a celebrity. On 13th April, Oscar appeared at the Tabor Opera House in the silver mining town of Leadville, Colorado where he talked about another silversmith, Benvenuto Cellini, to the miners. After the show, he rode down into the mine in a bucket where he officially opened a new shaft called "The Oscar" and dined with the miners:

"The first course was whiskey, the second whiskey and the third whiskey." The friendliness shown to Oscar by this unlikely audience was repeated throughout his life in his relationships with people from all walks of life.

Oscar was first and foremost a storyteller, a *seanachaidh*, (keeper of ancient Celtic storytelling traditions), a gift that enabled him to become a brilliant conversationalist. Renowned for his aphorisms, he once said: "We Irish are too poetical to be poets, but are the greatest talkers since the Greeks." His wit and humor were darted but rarely vindictive, his satire brilliant, his jokes amusing and frequently at his own expense. His world was made up of artists, writers, painters and high society with many personal friendships on both sides of the English channel; he was equally at home in London and Paris where he spoke flawless French.

In 1884, Oscar fell in love with Constance Lloyd, the daughter of a Dublin barrister, and chose her as his wife. Oscar loved Constance in his way, the early part of their marriage was happy, and he adored his two sons, Cyril and Vyvyan.

His one novel, *The Picture of Dorian Gray*, caused a major stir when it appeared in 1890. In this novel Oscar moved away from Aestheticism to a Decadent style which was popular in short fiction at the time using elaborate language to describe taboo subjects and favoring art and artifice over the natural world. Dorian, a beautiful young man "with a face like ivory and rose leaves" has his portrait painted and prays that he may remain as beautiful as his portrait, while the portrait will reflect the changes wrought by age. His wish comes true. Dorian immerses himself in all manner of excesses and finally, years later, confronts the portrait, hidden away in his attic and sees, to his horror, that the face in the portrait has become that of a grotesque satyr, while he remains forever young. Tragedy, of course, ensues. This book was criticized as unclean and poisonous, homoerotic, and decadent and did little to stop the rumors circulating about Oscar's sexual orientation and talk about the constant stream of young, male companions he hosted at London's best restaurants.

In 1891, Oscar met Lord Alfred Douglas, youngest son of the Marquess of Queensberry and known to Oscar and posterity as Bosie. At the time Bosie was an undergraduate at Oxford. Attracted to the beautiful, blonde young man, Oscar offered to coach him – and fell in love. Their affair was tempestuous, flamboyant, flagrant, and dangerous. Bosie was spoiled, self-centered, vindictive and reckless, yet Oscar indulged his every whim. In this grand passion, neither Oscar nor Bosie could be away from each other for long though, as time passed, Bosie became increasingly critical of Oscar, writing him "revolting" and "loathsome" letters. Bosie wrote poetry and even translated Oscar's *Salomé* from its original French into English. This was to become the source of Richard Strauss's opera, *Salomé*.

Bosie introduced Oscar to "renters," London's young male prostitutes, some of whom blackmailed their clients. Later, in *De Profundis*, Oscar would write: "It was like feasting with panthers, the danger was half the excitement." Oscar now led a triple life, as a writer, as a brilliant shining light in London's drawing rooms and in dark dens of iniquitous pleasure, attracted to breaking the rules for the thrills they provided. He wrote: "Every impulse we strive to strangle broods in the mind and poisons us .... the only way to get rid of a temptation is to yield to it."

The glamorous, scandalous pair Oscar and Bosie, along with their companions, were much talked about. Oscar was both extravagant and generous with money when he had it, entertaining friends royally, always a loyal and true friend. As a consequence of his new lifestyle however, Oscar rarely went home to his family. Constance, it seems, was dimly aware of what was going on, but she loved Oscar and turned a blind eye. Some of Oscar's long term friends such as Robbie Ross, whom Oscar had first met at Oxford, and Frank Harris, who published his earliest works, both stood by Oscar through the good and the bad years, and both were a major source of support and friendship to Constance. Another special friend of Oscar in these years was Ada Leverson, a writer and woman with a great heart.

The crisis began when the Marquess of Queensberry, Bosie's father, started to publicly deride Oscar calling him offensive names. In an infamous insult, the vindictive Marquess left an open card at Oscar's club with the words: "For Oscar Wilde posing sodomite." Further, the Marquess planned to attend the first night of *The Importance of Being Earnest* and to throw a bouquet of rotten turnips at the author at the curtain call. Fortunately, Oscar heard about this and was able to have the Marquess barred from the theatre. Ignoring all the warning signs and the advice of his friends, Oscar decided to take the Marquess to court for libel. Hating his father, Bosie used Oscar to take revenge on him for criticizing his lifestyle. The Marquess welcomed the chance to have a platform from which he could accuse Oscar openly of corrupting his son. The Court found the Marquess not guilty but so much had been revealed about Oscar's lifestyle that now he found himself in the dock accused of gross indecency, a crime under the laws of Britain at the time.

Oscar, the opera, begins here, on the day before Oscar Wilde is to be sentenced. The Santa Fe Opera presents the world premiere in the 2013 season. In the premiere performances countertenor David Daniels, a longtime friend of the composer, sings Oscar. Dwayne Croft sings

Walt Whitman, William Burden is Frank Harris, and Heidi Stober, the only woman in the cast, sings Ada. Reed Luplau is the dancer who portrays Bosie. Evan Rogister conducts and Kevin Newbury directs. *Oscar* is a co-commission and co-production with The Opera Company of Philadelphia where the opera will be presented in 2015.

Desirée Mays would like to thank the composer Theodore Morrison and his co-librettist John Cox for sharing their background comments and for permission to print their copyrighted synopsis in its entirety. Here are their words:

Oscar Wilde was "an unfinished sketch of a great man and showed great courage and manhood amid the collapse of his fortunes." These words were uttered by William Butler Yeats a century ago, and they seem true enough when offered by one of Oscar's younger contemporaries, but not quite enough to support his fullness as a man for the ages. The enormous myth that has developed since Yeats spoke on the subject has propelled Oscar to a level of importance and celebrity beyond that which his own spectacular imagination might have estimated. In recent years, new biographies, theater pieces, and scholarly contributions have refocused the public's attention on an artistic figure bound certainly for immortality. Our opera firmly places him there at the beginning along with Walt Whitman, who acts as commentator and witness at various points throughout the drama. During Oscar's American lecture tour in 1882 he paid a visit to Walt at home in Camden, New Jersey, where the two poets became friends. Oscar later said, "He is the grandest man I have ever seen, the simplest, most natural, and strongest character I have ever met in my life. I regard him as one of those wonderful, large, entire men who might have lived in any age and is not peculiar to any people."

Oscar returned to London where, in a very short time, he became one of the greatest comic playwrights ever in the English language. He also produced a large corpus of poetry, novels, children's stories, journalism, criticism, and essays on aesthetics and politics. He was happily married and the doting father of two sons. He invented the role of celebrity as we know it today, and by 1895 with *The Importance of Being Earnest* he was probably the most famous man in England. Three months later, he was totally ruined.

The opera portrays Oscar Wilde as one who constantly tempted fate to his own destruction, while at the same time entertaining everyone around him. He was incomparably brilliant with words and ideas, especially in spontaneous conversation, but also frequently unable to respond to life-changing events with clarity and solid judgment. Witness his self-destructive relationship with Lord Alfred Douglas (Bosie), and his inability to conceive of losing in his trials at the Old Bailey. Even though his trusted friends urged him not to bring a libel suit against Bosie's father, the Marquess of Queensberry, he brought the suit anyway, lost that battle in court, but refused to flee to France to avoid prosecution by the Crown for "gross indecency." His friend and biographer, Frank Harris, who knew him well, believed he was caught in a state of inertia in which he was simply unable to act on his own behalf. Neil McKenna's biography, *The Secret Life of Oscar Wilde*, makes a strong case that we embrace: Wilde was a man of immense intellectual, artistic and personal heroism who offers us an irresistible model for understanding our own potential for courage in the face of prejudice and hatred.

Underlying all his risk-taking was found a large degree of generous sensibility, and often pathos. In the prison scenes of Act II, as Oscar learns true compassion from and for his fellow inmates, the drama will reach a turning point. Near the end of the opera, in a conversation with Ada Leverson, there is a reawakening of optimism in our hero as he prepares to move to France to become an artist in exile. History observes, however, that he would write practically nothing else but his epic poem, *The Ballad of Reading Gaol*, a masterpiece. When asked later why he no longer wrote, Oscar replied: "Because

I have written all there was to write. I wrote when I did not know life; now that I do know the meaning of life, I have no more to write. Life cannot be written; life can only be lived. I have lived."

The events of the opera are not historically ordered but nevertheless occurred at some point during Oscar's three trials or at his four prisons. The timings and juxtapositions of these events are the responsibility of the authors. Most of the text in our libretto is drawn from words spoken or written by Oscar Wilde himself and his contemporaries. These are found in direct accounts of conversations, letters and other documents from a wide variety of sources. The connective tissue is ours.

CHARACTERS

Oscar Wilde, a countertenor
Max Beerbohm said that Oscar Wilde had a "mezzo voice, uttering itself in leisurely fashion, with every variety of tone." His perfect sentences seemed to Yeats to have been written 'overnight with labour and yet all spontaneous.' The title role for David Daniels is designed to reflect and elaborate upon this information, and indeed, David has been our inspiration for the role and the opera.

Walt Whitman, a baritone
Whitman died on 26 March, 1892, the very spring during which Oscar and Bosie Douglas became lovers. He is portrayed as commentator from the vantage point of immortality, observing Oscar on his journey to the same place. Whitman carried out in his writing and his life a critical examination of the ethics of his society in America that parallels with its own distinctive voice Wilde's similar work in London.

Ada Leverson, a soprano
Oscar called Leverson "Sphinx" and "the wittiest woman in the world." Behind her frivolous façade lay immense integrity

and moral strength. She and her husband bravely provided sanctuary for Oscar in their home while he was out on bail during his trials when he was rejected by almost all of London society and at every hotel. As a novelist later, she was highly regarded. Ada was amongst the first of Oscar's close friends to see him on the day of his release from prison. A party-loving night owl who always slept late (like Oscar), she arose before dawn that day for the sole purpose of going to greet her great friend.

Frank Harris, a tenor
Frank Harris was the author of a controversial biography of Oscar Wilde, but one that was supported by George Bernard Shaw, and in recent years by Merlin Holland, Oscar Wilde's grandson. By age thirty Harris edited the *Fortnightly Review*, and soon became owner and editor of the *Saturday Review*. In these positions he was at the center of the literary Nineties. Max Beerbohm called Harris "the best talker in London," an astonishing statement from a friend of Oscar Wilde. Frank spent some time in prison himself on behalf of a free press. He was always kind and generous to Oscar, whom he loved and admired.

Lord Alfred Douglas ("Bosie"), a dancer
Bosie was at once Wilde's lodestar and nemesis. He became the object of Oscar's deepest love, but it was he who introduced him to the world of male prostitution, which became Oscar's undoing. He moved to France at the beginning of the final trial and did not return to England during Wilde's two years in prison. The two men were often close after Wilde's release, but covertly. Throughout the opera Oscar evinces an almost pathological longing for Bosie, and at various stages of anguish or delirium conjures his presence in others – a French waiter, the prison doctor, Death, or as himself. Bosie's absence is powerful enough to give him, to Oscar, a palpable presence at all times, materializing at key moments in dance. A series of appropriate masks and

costumes for the dancer will enhance the images in keeping with Oscar Wilde's theory of masks: "Give a man a mask and he will tell you the truth."

Additional characters include Mr. Justice Sir Alfred Wills and Colonel Henry B. Isaacson. Wills was the "hanging judge" who presided at Oscar's final trial in the Old Bailey, and Isaacson was the malevolent and ruthless governor of Reading Gaol. He, like the judge, represents the cold voice of the Establishment. The two formidable detectives hired by Queensberry will harass Oscar and gather blameworthy information about him to be used at his trials. Two vicious prison warders torment Oscar in Reading Gaol, while one kind warder, Thomas Martin, provides him with friendship and comfort. There is a variety of smaller roles and chorus parts: participants in the trial, prisoners in Reading Gaol, and a host of immortals in the Epilogue.

ACT I

Prologue: In the regions of Immortality
Walt Whitman and Oscar Wilde manifest as immortals communicating from the fullness of their mythical personas. Walt introduces himself, and tells of his meeting with Oscar in America. Oscar sings about the honest nature of sorrow. Their shared prologue predicts the action that is to follow and offers philosophical underpinning for the story. Oscar concludes by addressing the audience: "What lies before you is my past."

Scene I: In the streets of London, 1895
With a backdrop of the looming, hostile city, Oscar is out on bail during his second trial for "gross indecency." (The first trial resulted in a hung jury.) He is followed by two menacing figures, Queensberry's detectives. Bosie, who has already slipped away to France, hates his father and has convinced Oscar that he will be found not guilty and his father humiliated.

Oscar goes from hotel to hotel, but wherever he attempts to register, the thugs intimidate the managers. At the end of the scene, Oscar, finally alone and dejected at having been turned away from every hotel, begins to ruminate on the serious nature of his plight. The walls of the city seem to cry out against him.

Scenes 2 - 7: In the home of Ada Leverson
Oscar finally turns to his friend Ada Leverson. Ada, whom Oscar calls Sphinx, offers him the nursery apartment in her home as a refuge. Through their initial conversation it becomes clear that she occupies a three-part presence in Oscar's life: as Sphinx she warns of the disaster bearing down upon him; as frequent companion and friend she offers good conversation; in a mothering role she brings him comfort and protection. Ada observes that Oscar's life with Bosie has been all frivolity and danger, and that Bosie, out of hatred for his father, has pressed Oscar to stay for trial against the urgent advice of his friends that he flee. She says that Frank Harris will soon arrive with a plan to help him escape. Hearing this, Oscar insists that they speak only of matters that are agreeable, not about his tribulations. Ada respects his request for respite, and Oscar reverts abruptly to light and entertaining conversation. He sings an aria that reveals some of his self-destructive inclinations. It describes how he went on a bender for three nights drinking absinthe in a French café. As a romantic fantasy, he sees a waiter watering the sawdust. This causes flowers to grow. The waiter's mask is removed revealing the image of Bosie who invites Oscar to dance. After Oscar tires, Bosie dances alone as Oscar watches. Bosie disappears. Oscar returns to consciousness and cries out in grief. Ada tries to comfort him.

Frank Harris is announced. Oscar leaves briefly to gird himself against what he knows will be Frank's strong persuasion to abscond to France. Ada greets Frank. The two of them engage in lively conversation during which Frank flirts with Ada. She responds with mischievous sarcasm. They become serious in the face of Oscar's situation, and Frank asks about her impressions of Oscar when she first met him. Ada describes how she expected a giant with the wings of a Brazilian butterfly, but she found him far more like a Roman emperor. When Oscar returns, Ada leaves the two men alone.

During an animated discussion in which Oscar tries to be as light-hearted as possible, Frank gravely and forcefully presses him to look at reality. Frank is convinced that there will be a guilty verdict and urges Oscar to jump bail. He offers him a means of escape on a borrowed yacht and suggests they should spend time travelling together. Oscar resists in an aria that teases Frank about his reputation as a social ruffian, but Frank, replying, reveals the sympathetic inner character that lies beneath his rowdy exterior.

Ada returns. Oscar tells her and Frank about his mother's chilling admonition that if he leaves she will never speak to him again. The friends interact in a trio in which Ada sings of her affection, Oscar of childhood, and Frank continues to predict darkly. They urge him to leave immediately, especially for the sake of his children. For the moment, Oscar seems convinced. Bosie appears and dances seductively in Oscar's imagination. He embraces Oscar as if to further influence his decision regarding flight. The incubus Bosie undoes with his sensuality all the good done by Ada and Frank. Bosie leaves. Oscar tells Ada and Frank that he has decided to stay. Frank says that he will stand by Oscar no matter what happens. Ada and Frank leave as Oscar, in a powerful soliloquy, declares his heroic resolve to stay for trial on behalf of "the love that dare not speak its name." Oscar leaves.

Walt Whitman appears and reflects that up to that point in Oscar's life his muse "had brought him brilliant and happy successes as an artist, as a man. But alas, it was not to continue. Nemesis had caught him in her net!" He asks sympathetically, "Why it is that a man runs to his own ruin? No one knows, but things are so. Can there be any heroes if the better angels of our nature always prevail, and can there be meaning to a life that feels no pain?" Returning, Oscar begins to compose a letter to Bosie as a means to clarify his mind and open his heart in preparation for his almost certain imprisonment. Walt reads the immortal text as Oscar writes. Bosie appears and dances to the spoken words (without orchestra). Oscar's imagination is set on fire. He sings an impassioned aria at the end of which he moves forward to embrace Bosie, but Queensberry's detectives arrive clamorously. In a comically black encounter they confront Bosie with studied hit-man politeness, warning him to leave England. Bosie, frightened, flees. The detectives turn viciously on Oscar. They fight. Oscar drives them from his fantasy and from the stage. The lights dim. Oscar is left alone in the dark calling in despair for Bosie.

It is the day of Oscar's conviction and sentencing. Ada receives an agitated Frank Harris who has been in court. He has promised to bring her immediate news of the verdict. In a diatribe he tells Ada about the events in the court just prior to Oscar's conviction and sentencing. Just as Frank reaches the point in his story at which the judge is about to ask for the verdict, the nursery explodes into a mockery of the Old Bailey trial. The action becomes farce as spectators, officials, judge and jury are depicted as malicious toys. Oscar is ushered in. Then the judge, chanting like a grotesque priest, asks the jury foreman for the verdict, which finds Oscar "guilty of gross indecency." This produces jubilation in the courtroom. The judge pronounces his malevolent sentence of two years at hard labour. Oscar asks, "And I, may I say nothing, my lord?" The judge screams, "Take him down!" Oscar is roughly and quickly removed from the court as pandemonium ensues among the spectators.

ACT II

Inside Reading Gaol

The prisoners bemoan their situation. Walt exhorts us to identify with them: "Each of these is one of us, and each of us is Oscar Wilde!" Oscar is pushed roughly into the receiving area of the prison, in chains. Two prison warders try to outdo each other by mocking him. Colonel Isaacson, the infamous governor of Reading Gaol, arrives with Quinton, the prison physician. Oscar looks frightened, but he comports himself with dignity and the intent to survive this humiliation. Isaacson lectures Oscar harshly on the rules of the prison and the punishments for any infringements, then leaves. The warders remove Oscar's chains, force him to strip off his fine clothes, and fumigate him. Quinton examines him; then he is made to put on a convict's uniform. Prisoners from their cells sing a strange and sorrowful chorale. Quinton watches from the background as Oscar's cell materializes at center stage. The warders bring Oscar his crank and order him to get to work, then leave. Oscar begins to turn the crank and sings a terrified aria. As the music slows, Oscar fantasizes about Bosie. Quinton begins to dance in the background. Collapsing, Oscar imagines Quinton is Bosie. The dance ends as Oscar reaches up to remove Quinton's mask, under which is Bosie's face, but coldly expressionless. Bosie vanishes.

On a Sunday morning months later the staff and prisoners attend chapel. Oscar is looking disheveled and ill. Taking advantage of the only chance to exercise their pent up voices, the men lustily sing a hymn. Midway, the Chaplain notices that Oscar has been sitting. He comes to Oscar, who somehow manages to stand. The Chaplain insults him. Now truly ill, Oscar falls and strikes his head. Doctor Quinton comes forward to examine him. Isaacson berates Oscar for malingering, but sends him to the infirmary as the prisoners become rebellious and are brought brutally to order by the warders.

In the evening Oscar and two other prisoners are seen lying in the infirmary. Walt Whitman observes the scene. Oscar, with a bandage on his head, surveys the room. He is somewhat dazed at first and sees the other prisoners with whom, at long last, he is able to have a friendly greeting. The men are sympathetic to Oscar. Martin, the benevolent warder, comes with a ward orderly to treat the prisoners. Trying to improve his own mind, Martin asks questions about literature to which Oscar is only too glad to respond. The men share jokes and laughter and risk a song. Their conversation helps to offer Oscar a little respite from the unrelenting gruesome routine. Martin bids the men goodnight. The men lament an impending execution. This scene initiates a pivotal point in Oscar's emotional perception of his situation, and a turning away from obsession with his own pain towards the greater suffering of others.

Night. The execution of Thomas Wooldridge will occur at dawn. The men await the hideous reality of the morning. The scene is highly fantastical and dream-like, the music stylized in response to the formal structure of the text, all of which is taken from *The Ballad of Reading Gaol*. This is principally an ensemble movement with Oscar Wilde as witness and Walt Whitman as commentator. Waiting through the long night hours, various configurations of voices sing stanzas. At a certain point the dancer comes as Death and releases the spirits of the prisoners from their captivity. They join in a Dance of Death. When the terrible red dawn arrives, the procession to the gallows begins. The clock strikes. Oscar sings an elegy to the hanged man:

> And all the woe that moved him so
>   That he gave that bitter cry,
> And the wild regrets, and the bloody sweats
>   None knew so well as I:
> For he who lives more lives than one
>   More deaths than one must die.

Weeks later Frank Harris brings Oscar the news that Isaacson is to be replaced as Governor by a man who is reputed to be kinder and fair. Oscar will be able to work outside in the garden and will have books and writing materials. Oscar looks increasingly hopeful. Frank urges Oscar to resume his writing. Oscar, over time, having begun to absorb into his nature all that his been done to him, declares that he will fight with his pen to change the prison system for the future victims of society's unjust laws and insane punishments. At that moment Isaacson struts into the room and sends Oscar back to his cell. He boasts to Frank that he has been "knocking the nonsense out of Wilde!" Frank responds with a volley of excoriating verbal cannon fire until Isaacson leaves. Martin comes to escort Frank from the prison as they both express their admiration of Oscar.

It is three days before Oscar's release. Ada is brought in by Martin to visit him. They meet in the prison garden and talk about family and friends. Ada declares that he will always be a legend and defines his certain place in the literary pantheon. Oscar has high hopes of being housed in a Jesuit seminary on his release, but Ada has to tell him that he has been rejected. Martin escorts Ada from the prison. Oscar watches them walk into the bright light of the setting sun. Bosie materializes in the same light. Oscar then sings a threnody based on lines from his prescient early poem, *Glukopikros Eros*, in which he accepts the blame for all that has happened. Bosie dances briefly between the vocal phrases. The aria ends with the text, "I have made my choice, have lived my poems, and though youth is gone in wasted days, I have found the lover's crown of myrtle better than the poet's crown of bays."

Epilogue: Immortality
A host of immortals arrives with Walt Whitman. Walt steps forward as Bosie and Oscar bid each other farewell. Bosie yields Oscar to Walt, then leaves. Oscar is vested in the raiment of the Immortals and takes his place on the threshold

of the House of Fame. Walt and Oscar sing Whitman's *Whispers of Heavenly Death*. Walt then takes Oscar by the hand and leads him across the threshold, introducing him to the company by his full name. The immortals respond with fanfares of "Oscar! Oscar!" Our hero embraces his immortality and ends the opera with a wink to the subject of immortality.

♪

Bibliography

Ellmann, Richard, *Oscar Wilde*. Alfred A. Knopf, New York, 1988.

McKenna, Neil, *The Secret Life of Oscar Wilde*. Basic Books, New York, 2005.

Maine, G.F. Edit., *The Works of Oscar Wilde*. Collins London and Glasgow, 1960.

Personal communications with Theodore Morrison and John Cox, December, 2012.

La Traviata

Giuseppe Verdi

She was a phantom of delight when first she gleamed upon my sight;
A lovely apparition sent to be a moment's ornament.
— William Wordsworth

"To be truly loved by a courtesan is difficult to achieve. In such women, the body has consumed the soul, the senses have burnt out the heart, debauchery has buckled stout armor onto feeling. The words you say, they first heard long ago; the tactics you use, they have seen before; the very love they inspire in you, they have sold to others. Love is their trade. But when God allows a courtesan to fall in love, her love, which at first looks like a pardon for her sins proves almost invariably to be a punishment on her. There is no absolution without penance." Thus wrote Alexandre Dumas *fils* at the end of his love affair with Marie Duplessis, the most beautiful courtesan in Paris in the late 1840s.

Violetta, an operatic character based on Duplessis' story, is classed as an upwardly mobile prostitute. Even the title of her opera, *La Traviata* or The Strayed One, suggests she has wandered off the straight and narrow with not one but many lovers. The plural is the problem: one lover, in or out of marriage, may have been acceptable, serial lovers were not. Opera is filled with examples of these fallen women: Carmen is viewed as a gypsy trollop, Madame Butterfly as a geisha prostitute, Lulu is a fully fledged scarlet woman.

Why is the playing field rarely even with the same set of moral standards for men as for women? Violetta Valéry, the gorgeous, consumptive, very young woman, epitomized the double standard of the Second Empire in France, specifically in Paris. There were rumblings of unhappy women in the French countryside also; think of Madame Bovary, for whom one of the few high points in her life was attending a performance of *La Traviata* and longing, from her own country-wife existence, to emulate the fascinating Violetta.

Who was Marie Duplessis, the courtesan, who triggered the creative imaginations of Alexandre Dumas *fils* in *La Dame aux Camélias* and Giuseppe Verdi in *La Traviata?* The Second Empire was a time of hedonistic pleasure in the history of France, a time when the golden age of the courtesan was at its peak in the early 19th century fading away with the onset of the Franco-Prussian war in 1870 and over by World War I. The extravagant world of the courtesan was known as the *demi-monde*, or half-world. Alexandre Dumas, who wrote of his famous affair with the courtesan Marie Duplessis, stated: "Though they have the same origin, the same appearance and the same prejudices as women of society, they do not belong to it: they constitute the *demi-monde* or half-world, a veritable floating island on the ocean of Paris.." In Verdi's opera, Violetta refers to this floating island as: "This crowded desert they call Paris."

Georges Sand, lover of Frédéric Chopin, wrote in her journal: "The satisfaction of a personal passion is pleasure or intoxication. It is not happiness. Happiness, to deserve the name, must be enduring and indestructible." Women had prescribed places in French society where they could survive – or not – either as servants; as self-employed workers eking out a living, like Mimi sewing hats in *La Bohème* and depending on bohemian lovers for added financial support; or as women of the upper classes, another form of kept woman, who did not work but who was expected to run her husband's household efficiently, raise his children and turn a blind eye whenever the topic of "mistress" came up. Aristocratic women were, in those days, more often than not victims of arranged marriages by their families in order to increase the family's influence, wealth or lands. Think of *Lucia di Lammermoor*. Any woman, from whatever class, who had the misfortune to love, have sex with and, God forbid, bear a child by a man outside of marriage was instantly condemned, dismissed, labeled as fallen, and cast out from her own society. In fact, many women of good families who became such victims constituted the peculiarly French world of the *demi-monde*, neither in nor out of society, women who were acceptable as lovers, companions and hostesses but certainly not in the drawing rooms of their lovers' families.

A new kind of woman, self-made, smart and beautiful, decided that two could play this game and if men wanted glamorous escorts they would have to pay in jewels, apartments, gorgeous clothes, furs, carriages and horses, some kind of insurance against the hard times. These women didn't care what people thought of them, they were too busy having a good time and wielding all kinds of unexpected influence behind the scenes. Many were the "favorites" of kings and princes. Men actually gained prestige in the eyes of their contemporaries by having a beautiful courtesan on their arm as a conspicuous symbol of affluence. Courtesans would be passed from man to man when their "protectors" grew bored with them, or when they were out of funds. When an affair had run its course for whatever reason, the benefactor simply stopped paying the bills and the courtesan moved on to another man. Some of the more fortunate ones married, finding an official protector in the married state. Marie Duplessis married a man who loved her, the Vicomte de Perregaux. His family refused to recognize the marriage but she kept the title, the Vicomtesse de Perregaux, and it was her husband who provided a grave for her in Montmartre cemetery at her death at the age of 23.

Maybe it is a factor of time. The very word "courtesan" originally referred to those who served at court, at the pleasure of the kings and nobles – literally. Thaïs, rumored to be the mistress of Alexander the Great, was immortalized in Massenet's opera; Theodora, an erotic actress dancer in 500 AD had an affair with Justinian, the Emperor. She became Empress on marrying him and when she died was canonized as a orthodox saint. Jane Shore in the early 15th century became the favorite of King Edward IV in England. He called her "the merriest, wiliest and holiest of harlots." The convent-educated Madame de Pompadour became mistress to Louis XV until her death when Madame du Barry took her place. But du Barry came to a bad end, guillotined by the mob in December 1793. Moving forward to the 20th century, Lily Langtry was an actress who became the mistress of England's Prince of Wales; Sarah Bernhardt was a courtesan before she established herself as the greatest actress of her time.

Marie Duplessis, who lived from 1824 to 1847, had a brutal childhood. She escaped her father and arrived in Paris at the age of 15, penniless and desperate. She became a seamstress, then was set up in her own apartment by a restauranteur. The elderly Comte de Stackelberg took an interest in her and provided her with an education, an apartment in the upscale Boulevard de la Madeleine, and the skills to be whatever she wanted to be in society. She had many wealthy and titled lovers, including Franz Liszt who adored her. The young Alexandre Dumas *fils* fell in love with her and they had a brief affair. Following her death he wrote her story, *La Dame aux Camélias*. With the publication of this book, Marie Duplessis was immortalized in literature as Marguerite Gautier, a novel read by everyone in Paris at the time. Giuseppe Verdi, seeing the Dumas play in Paris in 1852, only four years after Marie Duplessis' death, at once decided to write an opera about this fallen woman who, in Verdi's compassionate hands, was reborn as Violetta Valéry in *La Traviata*.

In his book, Dumas describes in detail the lifestyle of Marguerite Gautier and women like her. When he meets her at her house in Paris, he reports: "She was visibly still in the virgin stage of vice, her confident bearing, her large eyes faintly ringed with blue, all pointed to one of those passionate natures which give out a bouquet of sensuality. One could detect in this girl a virgin who had been turned into a courtesan by the merest accident of chance. At dinner we laughed and drank. Within minutes the merriment had sunk to the lowest level with witticisms of the kind which certain circles find so amusing and which never fail to defile the lips of those who utter them. This way of talking appeared in Marguerite to be a need to forget, a restlessness, a nervous reaction. With each glass of champagne her cheeks took on a feverish blush and a cough forced her head against the back of her chair, holding her chest with both hands each time the coughing seized her. She closed her eyes in pain and put her lips to a serviette which turned red with a splash of blood."

The fictional Armand, the alter ego of Alexandre, warns Marguerite she is killing herself and offers to take care of her. She tells him: "What keeps me going is the pace of the life I lead. Women like me are abandoned the moment we are of no more use for feeding the vanity or pleasure of our lovers, then long, empty evenings follow long, empty days." Marguerite tries to warn off her young impetuous admirer, describing herself as "temperamental, ill, depressed or gay in a way that is sadder than sorrow itself, someone who coughs blood and who spends 100,000 francs a year." But eventually she tells him she will be his if he promises to be "trusting, submissive and discreet." She wants the freedom to be her own mistress and not to be at the mercy of a protector. But Armand is in love, he does not listen.

Prudence, Marguerite's friend in Dumas' book, tells him exactly what the life of a courtesan entails: "How do you imagine the kept women in Paris could carry on living the kinds of lives they lead if they didn't have three or four lovers at the same time? Marguerite is lucky, she has a rich old man whose wife and daughter are dead, he gives her everything she wants. If Marguerite gave up the Count and the Duke for you, what sacrifice could you make to match hers? When you'd had enough of her you would cut her off from the world in which her fortune and her future lay. She would have given you her best years, and she would be forgotten."

Marguerite herself explains the realities of her lifestyle to her young lover: "We creatures of chance have weird desires and unimaginable passions. There are men who would ruin themselves for us and get nowhere, there are others who can have us for a bunch of flowers. Naturally we have no friends. We have egotistical lovers who spend their fortunes not on us, as they claim, but on their vanity. Our lives are no longer our own. We aren't human beings but things."

And this is the young woman we meet in the opening

scene of Giuseppe Verdi's *La Traviata*, Violetta Valéry, the hostess of a lively party. Her benefactor Baron Douphol watches nonchalantly from a distance; it is the young Alfredo Germont, just arrived in Paris who, on his first visit to the courtesan's house, provides the toast to the sparkling Violetta. She is attracted to the lovesick young man and, in the long finale of the first act, Violetta tries to sort out her feelings. Alone on stage, she sings of the transience of her lifestyle: "Let us enjoy life for the pleasures of love are swift and fleeting as a flower that lives and dies and can be enjoyed no more" (Sempre libera). Knowing she is dying of consumption she is determined to squeeze every last drop out of life in the short time she has. But under the frivolous exterior Violetta knows her lifestyle is superficial and cannot provide her with lasting happiness; she also knows that her illness places her under a sentence of early death. Tuberculosis (TB) or consumption was little understood in the mid-1800s; the cause of the illness was not discovered until the latter part of the century, and the cure was not known until 1943 with the discovery of streptomycin. There were a lot of misconceptions, old wives' tales about TB in Marie Duplessis' time. In 1853, a medical text stated: "Of all the vices none are so apt to lead to consumption as the unnatural or unrestrained indulgence of the sensual passions." So, if a courtesan contracted the disease, the thinking was that it was to be expected. TB was believed to be an aphrodisiac which conferred special powers of seduction on its victims. The consumptive young woman was described as having pale white skin with flushed cheeks, large dark luminous eyes and red lips, this was the "look" of the romantic heroine to whom men were, for some perverse reason, irredeemably attracted. An English study from 1844 showed that the disease was out of control and was the leading cause of death in the population. The very Prelude of the opera, beautiful and ethereal, describes tuberculosis, suggesting death is not far off for the frail Violetta.

When she meets Alfredo, a young man of no means who could never be her benefactor and provide her with the luxury she enjoys, she wonders if this could be different: "Does he love me? I, who have never loved anyone. Who am I? We women always imagine we will be loved, never that we shall be in love ourselves so that at the first assault of this unforeseen trouble we do not know where we are." In the long *scena* at the end of the first act she imagines being in love. Alfredo's voice is heard offstage singing of the pain and delight of love (croce e delizia). Violetta listens, dreaming, then shakes herself from her reverie; it cannot be. How can she dream of love, a poor girl lost in the great city of Paris? Why should she give up the pleasure she craves? She sings a thrilling aria reaching ever higher and higher as she feverishly tries to convince herself that this is what she truly wants.

In the second act she has changed her mind and we see her living blissfully and simply with Alfredo in a villa on the outskirts of Paris. They are completely happy, until reality makes itself felt with the necessity of paying the bills for their love nest and with the arrival of Alfredo's puritanical father, Germont. Now we see another side of the brilliant courtesan. She has left the wild life of Paris and, happy with Alfredo, chooses to sell her belongings to support their life in the country, but he will not hear of this and rushes off to Paris to raise funds. His father, Germont, arrives in Alfredo's absence and tells Violetta he will not hear of his son marrying a courtesan. In the pivotal scene in the opera, Germont ultimately forces Violetta to his point of view when he tells her that his daughter's impending marriage will be called off if her fiancé's family learn that Alfredo is considering marriage to a courtesan. This long duet of psychological twists and turns is heartbreaking as Violetta is beaten down by the force of Germont's arguments. Where society tolerated men who had mistresses, they crossed the line if they married. Violetta, the courtesan, will not sacrifice Alfredo's sister so she agrees to leave her lover, her one chance of happiness and indeed of survival. Alfredo returns to the villa and the grief- stricken Violetta passionately assures him she loves him: "Amami, Alfredo" (Love me as I love you), her final words to her lover before she flees. She takes the only path open to her as a courtesan and returns to her former debilitating lifestyle and her protector, Baron Douphol.

The naively passionate Alfredo pursues her to Paris and arrives at the ball where she appears on the arm of the Baron. In a jealous rage he grossly slanders and insults the woman he loves by throwing money at her feet saying: "For all that she had spent on me, now I repay the debt I owe." The public insult to Violetta is one from which she cannot recover and soon afterwards her consumption forces her to her bed and death.

Alfredo fought a duel with the Baron, left Paris until the fuss died down, but then, on receiving a letter from his father about Violetta's sacrifice, he returns in time for the death scene, for the final duet, as must happen in opera. In Dumas' book, Marguerite dies alone, hoping to see her lover every time the door to her room opens. A maid, who loved her, kept a diary of her final days describing terrible suffering with creditors hovering nearby and still her lover did not come. When, at last, he did arrive back in Paris she had already been buried. He visited her grave before being welcomed back into the heart of his family.

Verdi always loved this opera even though it "was a fiasco," his words, at its first performance in Venice in 1853.

He and Giuseppina Strepponi, the woman he loved and whom he married six years later, were living at his home Sant'Agata, not far from Busseto, in these years. Verdi travelled alone to Rome for the premiere of *Il Trovatore* in July, 1852 and was happy with the "total triumph" of this opera. Strepponi was not with him for this triumph and, though always supportive, she was bored in his absence and wrote: "If I could see you for a quarter of an hour out of every 24, I would be in high spirits, would work, read, write and time would pass quickly."

Verdi and Strepponi were at home when Francesco Piave, the librettist who had worked with Verdi on other operas, joined them to work with the maestro on the libretto of *La Traviata*, which was outlined in five days. Verdi always sought subjects that were in his words, "new, great, beautiful and daring in the extreme with new forms." His choice of *La Dame aux Camélias* for *La Traviata* a contemporary subject, was certainly that. The management of La Fenice in Venice where the opera was to be given, on hearing that it was to be about a courtesan who had died only a few years earlier, insisted the time frame be set back at least 100 years. Verdi was upset at this decision since the whole point of the opera was that it was contemporary to his time. He was also far from happy about the management's choice of singers. Using his rheumatism as an excuse, he threatened to pull out if the right singer with "an elegant figure, young, who can sing passionately" could not be found to sing Violetta. By February 1853, *La Traviata* was in rehearsal at La Fenice. Only then was the libretto sent to the censors. Verdi was not allowed to present his opera in contemporary costumes and period. Also he was getting reports that the singers were far from good and was warned of "inevitable disaster." Verdi arrived in Venice on February 21 and worked on the orchestrations while Piave led the rehearsals. Finally, with a cast Verdi did not want and a setting in the time of Louis XIV which Verdi did not want either, the premiere took place on March 6. The Prelude and the first act were applauded, but the rest was the predicted disaster. Neither the singers nor the audience understood what the opera was about, especially in period costumes when the whole concept of courtesans didn't make sense. Verdi himself reported: "A fiasco. Is it my fault or the singers? Time will tell." A year later, on May 6, at another theatre in Venice and with an entirely new cast, *La Traviata* played with extraordinary success. Ricordi, Verdi's music publisher, wrote to him: "There was such an uproar of indescribable applause! There was never a success in Venice like that of *La Traviata*." The opera continued to be given in a Louis XIV setting as late as 1906 when it became contemporary to Verdi's time of 1853, the time of the courtesans of the Second Empire, as he intended.

It is amazing that Verdi composed *Il Trovatore* and *La Traviata* concurrently when they are so different in mood and temperament, one virile and expansive, the other feminine and intimate. The Prelude that opens *La Traviata* is unique, a description of Violetta from the strings in a poignant melody that recurs as she is dying; the figure of death hangs over this young woman from the opening bars of the opera. Then the music bursts into an effervescent waltz as Violetta greets and flirts with her guests. Her long solo aria and cabaletta at the end of the first act tests the soprano with its many changing moods, colors and sheer virtuosity. The tenor's aria comes at the start of Act II in complete contrast to what has come before; he sings of his love and joy of being with Violetta away from Paris and its frenetic pace of life. The duet between Germont and Violetta is the dramatic heart of the opera in a brilliant musical tug of war which Germont ultimately wins. The aria that ends the act is Germont's when he pleads with his now heartbroken son to return home with him to Provence, "Di Provenza il mar." In Act II sc.ii, at the party in Paris where Violetta arrives with the Baron, the music ratchets up the emotions of everyone on stage describing the flirtation of the courtesans with their lovers; the condescending attitude of the Baron with the lovely, though suffering Violetta, on his arm; her terrified confusion at seeing Alfredo at the party when in her heart she longs to be with him and would be but for the promise she made his father; Alfredo's extreme fury and jealousy which results in his losing his temper and throwing money at Violetta and then, finally, the appearance of Germont, his father, who castigates his son: "Disgraceful outrage! You shame a woman." The music encompasses these many violent emotions and the audience is left breathless by the end of the act.

The final act is calm, the music of the Prelude returns, it is time for Violetta to die, the disease has run its course. Alone but for the doctor and her faithful maid, Violetta is dying. As she suffers, we too wait and pray for Alfredo's return and with him, are devastated by the realization that he comes too late, Violetta is leaving her pain behind. Yet it is here, in the final moments of the opera, that some of Verdi's most beautiful music is heard: Violetta's "Addio, del passato" (Farewell, happy dreams of the past) when she realizes death is near, and then the heart-breaking "Parigi, o cara" (Let us leave Paris, beloved) when she is, for a last few moments, held in Alfredo's arms as they dream together of what might be. All of these conflicting heart-rending moments are played out in Verdi's extraordinarily sensitive score.

The Santa Fe production begins, in the sombre Prelude, with men carrying a coffin on their shoulders in the rain to its final resting place. The open black umbrellas are like dark wings that would hide from us the story of Violetta, but the music will not let that be as it bursts into a fevered waltz of happy partygoers and we are cast back into Violetta's last months of life in a glittering scene of mirrors, wine and song. Violetta is the belle of the ball who takes a chance on love, finds it cannot work for her, loses the one man she truly did love and dies.

The Santa Fe production reprises the insightful interpretation of director Laurent Pelly, with conductor Leo Hussain on the podium. The cast is one of young award-winning singers: Brenda Rae as Violetta, Michael Fabiano as Alfredo and Roland Wood as Germont, the father.

♪

Characters

Violetta Valery	Soprano
Alfredo Germont	Tenor
Giorgio Germont, his father	Baritone
Baron Douphol	Baritone

Bibliography

Dumas, Alexandre fils. *La Dame aux Camélias*. Oxford University Press, 1986

Griffin, Susan. *The Book of the Courtesans*. Broadway Books, New York, 2001.

John, Nicholas, ed., *La Traviata, Giuseppe Verdi*. English National Opera Guide 5, Riverrun Press, New York, 1981.

Richardson, Joanna. *The Courtesans: The Demi-Monde in 19th Century France*. Phoenix Press, London, 1967.

Voi che sapete che cosà è amor...

The Marriage of Figaro: Cherubino, the Countess and Susanna

The Marriage of Figaro

Wolfgang Amadeus Mozart

The overture to *The Marriage of Figaro* contains none of the music in the opera, but it anticipates an evening of mischief and intrigue which explores a favorite topic of Mozart's, the war of the sexes. The mercurial lightness of the overture dances its way into the opening scene in which Figaro, valet to Count Almaviva, is discussing wedding plans with his fiancée, Susanna. What could be simpler?

It was said of Caron de Beaumarchais, the playwright who created Figaro, that he had but one character – Figaro, who was himself. A wit and an adventurer, Beaumarchais fought against injustice in the days prior to the French Revolution. He wrote a series of three plays: *Le Barbier de Séville* (1775), *La Folle Journée ou Le Mariage de Figaro* (1784), and *La Mère Coupable* (The Guilty Mother) (1797). *Le Mariage* was banned by Louis XVI, who saw social criticism in Beaumarchais's impertinent text. It was not until the intercession of his wife, Marie Antoinette, that permission was granted for its performance. Napoleon later described the play as "revolution in action."

Lorenzo da Ponte, the colorful librettist with whom Mozart collaborated on his three greatest operas – *Le Nozze di Figaro*, *Così fan Tutte*, and *Don Giovanni* – first met Mozart in Vienna, when the two men discussed the possibility of making Beaumarchais's *Figaro* into an opera. Since the Emperor, Joseph II, had banned all performances of the play, both knew that an opera based on it would run into censorship problems. As Poet to the Imperial Theatres, da Ponte went to Joseph and assured him, "I have written an opera, not a comedy, and I have left out anything which might offend the delicacy and decency of an entertainment at which your Majesty might preside. As to [Mozart's] music, it is remarkably beautiful." Joseph invited Mozart to play the music for him and, realizing that da Ponte was right, allowed the opera to go ahead.

Mozart's collaboration with da Ponte was one of magical proportions. In 1781 Mozart had written to his father, "In an opera the poetry must be altogether the obedient daughter of the music." Da Ponte was willing to be subordinate to Mozart's greater intellectual depth and understanding of the theatre. His own great contributions were good craftsmanship, wit, excellent plot construction, graceful verse, and insightful characterization.

The première was held in Vienna in 1786 and was successful; later the same year it played in Prague, where it caused a sensation. Mozart reported, "Here they talk of nothing but *Figaro*. Nothing is played, sung, or whistled but *Figaro*. No opera is drawing audiences like *Figaro*. Certainly a great honor for me" (January 1787). Brahms said of the opera, "Each number is a miracle."

Mozart communicates on many levels; *Figaro* is a true marriage of words and music, a Mozartian world in which a marriage of true love is also a marriage of true minds. He presents a musical language in which certain keys describe certain emotions: F minor represents sadness and lament; A major is the key of young love; G minor hints at illicit sex. Puns and jokes are heard in the music; when, for instance,

Figaro describes the horns on the heads of cuckolded men, the French horns echo his words.

Called an "Opera Buffa in Four Acts," *Figaro* is set during the course of one crazy day (*"La Folle Journée"*) near Seville. There are eleven characters, more than was usual for the Court Opera. The soprano Nancy Storace, of Italian/British birth, sang Susanna at the première. Due to difficulties with her top notes, Mozart scored all of Susanna's music low; so low that today the role is generally sung by mezzo-sopranos.

An Irish tenor, Michael Kelly (or, as he called himself in Europe, Michele Ochelli), doubled the roles of Basilio and the lawyer, Don Curzio. Kelly reported at the time, "Mozart was on stage in his crimson pelisse and gold-laced cocked hat, giving time to the orchestra. Benucci [Figaro] gave *"Non più andrai"* with the greatest animation and power of voice. Mozart, *sotto voce*, was repeating, "Bravo! Bravo! Benucci!" The musicians applauded, beating their bows against the music desks. "The little man acknowledged, by repeated bows, his thanks for the enthusiastic applause."

The stage manager, Bussani, doubled the roles of Dr. Bartolo and the gardener, Antonio, with a very fast costume change. His wife sang the first Cherubino with difficulty because she could not remember the part. The young page is scored for a soprano; even in the Beaumarchais play, Cherubino was to be played by a young woman. Mozart smuggled a 12-year-old German girl into the theatre to sing the role of Barbarina. Five years later, this young girl sang the first Pamina in *The Magic Flute*.

It is interesting how the three plays of Beaumarchais evolved over time: from his *Barber of Seville* (1775) to composer Paisiello's *Barber* in 1782, to Rossini's great *Barber of Seville* in 1816. Beaumarchais's *Le Mariage de Figaro* was immortalized in Mozart's opera in 1786. His third play, *La Mère Coupable*, became an opera by Darius Milhaud in 1966, but has not remained in the repertoire. The most contemporary treatment of Beaumarchais is John Corigliano's 1991 *Ghosts of Versailles*, which features Beaumarchais himself, Marie Antoinette, and the children of *La Mère Coupable.*

The opening-night audience at *The Marriage of Figaro* in Vienna in May 1786 would have known that Count Almaviva was a nobleman of Seville, and the highest judge in Andalusia. About to be sent as ambassador for Spain to England, he is a man of some importance. In *The Barber of Seville*, Almaviva, bored with life in Madrid, goes to Seville to pursue a young woman with whom he has fallen in love. The young woman, Rosina, is a ward of Dr. Bartolo, who has his own plans to marry her. With the help of Figaro, the general factotum, and the mischievous Rosina, Bartolo is outwitted and the Count and Rosina escape, marry, and, one presumes, live happily ever after.

That is, until *The Marriage of Figaro*, which is set some three years after *The Barber of Seville.* The Count, bored now with married life, seeks diversion, and thinks he has found it on his doorstep with Susanna, his wife's maidservant. His wife, Rosina, the Countess, is not entirely comfortable in her new role as a lady and is unhappy over her spouse's dalliances. Her friend, the barber Figaro, now promoted to the Count's valet, plans marriage to Susanna. Dr. Bartolo is retained in the Count's household, as is Marcellina, the onetime governess of Rosina who is now housekeeper to the Count. Basilio, the scurrilous music teacher from *The Barber of Seville*, still provides music and, more important, acts as liaison between the philandering Count and the women he desires.

The opera begins with a domestic scene as Susanna explains to the somewhat slow Figaro that the proximity of their room to the Count's means that the Count plans to "Bribe me to grant him his feudal right as lord and master on the night of our wedding." *Le droit du Seigneur* was a feudal custom whereby the Lord had the right to have sex with his vassal's bride-to-be on the eve of the wedding. This medieval tradition was never actually law, but it was an ugly practice that servants were powerless to prevent. In reality, the custom was brought to an end long before *Figaro*. It was Beaumarchais who had the Count rescind his right saying, "The abolition of a shameful custom is no more than an acknowledgment of what is due to common decency." Now he is having second thoughts, for he plans to possess Susanna before the wedding night. To this end he has promised the couple a dowry and a bedroom close to his. Susanna, however, has a mind of her own, and will not comply. The Count is constantly frustrated as she persists in denying him her favors; in this, Almaviva and Don Giovanni are alike, for neither man succeeds in his pursuit of women in either opera.

Almaviva, an aristocrat who is used to getting his way without question, is confused and frustrated at every turn: Susanna will not have him, Figaro is impertinent, and the young page, Cherubino, seems to be underfoot every time he approaches a woman. In the double standard of the time it was acceptable for the Count to be unfaithful, but the same did not hold true for his wife. When Almaviva thinks that Rosina is possibly having an affair, he is furious, jealous, his honor at stake. Almaviva is manipulated by all the major characters in the plot, outwitted at every turn by his servants and even by his wife. Unaware of the extent to which he is made to look a fool, he continues blindly in the old ways, unforgiving and stubborn. The Count's sole aria, at the beginning of the third act, comes when it seems Susanna will not succumb and he rages against what he perceives to be the injustice of it all, *"Vedro mentr'io sospiro:"*

> *Must I see a serf of mine happy, while I am left to sigh?*
> *Must I see her who roused in me a passion*
> *United by the hand of love to a slave?*
> *You were not born, bold fellow, [Figaro] to cause me torment*
> *And laugh at my discomfort.*

The Countess, Rosina, first appears alone in her rooms at the start of the second act. She sings of the loss of her husband's love in a cavatina, *"Porgi, amor,"* "Give me back my loved one or, in mercy, let me die." Isolated by her marriage and abandoned by her husband, Rosina is no longer the vital, mischievous young woman of *The Barber of Seville.* She is distanced and set apart, confiding only in her maid, Susanna, and Figaro. Yet a sense of fun has not entirely left Rosina, for she welcomes the attentions of Cherubino, the young page, who loves her, wears her ribbon, and composes love songs to her. When cornered in a compromising situation (she and Susanna are dressing Cherubino as a woman), the Countess stands her ground as her husband unexpectedly knocks at the door and demands to be let in.

Ignoring the social conventions that made them mistress and servant, Rosina and Susanna are good friends. The two women refuse to become rivals sexually jealous of one another because of the Count's behavior. The strength of their alliance gives the opera a poignancy that is rare. In 1786, these two women, mistress and maid, stood together united against the tyranny of the Count and the ways of the *ancien régime.*

Rosina can be portrayed either as an abandoned woman or as a woman who fights for what she believes in, for it is she, not Figaro, who devises the plan to bring the Count to his knees begging forgiveness. She dictates a letter to Susanna suggesting the Count meet Susanna in the garden later that night, only the woman he will meet will not be Susanna but the Countess herself dressed in her maid's clothes. In a lovely duet, the Countess dictates, "How sweet the breeze will be this evening in the pine-grove." "The pine-grove?" Susanna queries. "He'll understand," Rosina assures her. In lieu of a seal, the two women affix the note with a pin from the Countess's lapel.

The Countess hesitates momentarily at the audacity of her plan; she is taking a risk, and she is not comfortable, "To what humiliation am I reduced by a cruel husband who, after loving me, then neglected and deceived me, in a strange mixture of infidelity, jealousy, and disdain, now forces me to seek help from my servants?" She reminisces, in one of opera's loveliest arias, *"Dove sono,"* "Where are those happy moments of sweetness and pleasure? If only my constancy in loving him always could bring hope of changing his ungrateful heart." But she goes through with the plan and, in the end, when the Count is made to realize, before his entire assembled staff, that the woman he was making love to in the arbor was not Susanna but his wife, he is at last contrite and begs forgiveness. The final measures of the opera are Rosina's moments of sheer transcendence as she forgives her errant husband.

Figaro is the figurehead who makes this opera revolutionary; he is the servant who, along with Susanna, the Countess, and Cherubino, challenges the system on behalf of servants, women, and the young respectively. All three triumph over the dissolute Count.

Figaro is the same jaunty character we met in *The Barber of Seville*, but in *The Marriage of Figaro* his plans come to naught; everything backfires. He attempts to have the Count perform a little ceremony of placing the symbol of purity, a crown of orange blossoms and its white veil, on Susanna's head, but his master keeps putting him off. He sends the Count an anonymous note stating that the Countess has an assignation that night with a lover, but that misfires. At the start, he has no idea that the Count has designs on his Susanna until she tells him and, at the end, he has no idea of who is meeting whom in the arbors in the garden.

Yet Figaro, sung by the beloved bass Benucci at the première, sings three of the opera's great arias. In the first he addresses the Count mockingly as "little Count," (*"Se vuol ballare, Signor Contino,"*): "If, my dear Count, you feel like dancing, it's I who'll call the tune." Figaro expresses his determination in this little cavatina set to an aristocratic minuet. He ends the first act with a lively march, *"Non più andrai,"* painting a painful picture of war to Cherubino, who has been flirting with Susanna and who has just been banished to the army: "No more, you amorous butterfly, will you go fluttering round night and day."

In the last act, Figaro mistakenly believes that Susanna has indeed agreed to meet the Count, and he vents his anger and frustration in an extraordinary musical portrait of jealousy in *"Aprite un po'quegl' occhi,"*: "Open your eyes, you rash and foolish men, and look at these women, and see them as they are." This is another instance of the double standard that prevailed in which women were seen as fickle, while men could act exactly as they chose. Even Basilio reiterates this fact when he sings, *"Così fan tutte le belle!"* "All women act like that." This line, *"Così fan tutte,"* went on to become the title of Mozart and da Ponte's next opera, with the self-same melody appearing in *Cosi*'s overture.

Susanna, arguably the central character, is the only truly virtuous person in the opera. Living by her wits, she manages to sidestep the Count's advances by telling both Figaro and the Countess about his overtures. She loves Figaro and will be married to him. She is faithful to her mistress, the Countess, as both her confidante and partner in planning the exposure of the Count's indiscretions. Susanna is filled with a *joie de vivre* that Mozart so tellingly brings to life in her music. On stage for most of the opera, she interacts with the other characters in duets and ensembles. Her aria in the last act is one of the great testimonies to love when she sings, accompanied by strings, flute, oboe, and bassoon, *"Deh vieni, non tardar,"* ("Do not delay, oh bliss, come where love calls thee to joy"). The mood is one of ecstatic tranquility and harmony. For the singer, however, this aria, coming near the end of four long acts, is a major test; the voice will certainly be warmed up, but the singer may be exhausted.

Cherubino, a new member of the cast of since *The Barber*, is a page to the Count. He calls the Countess his godmother for, as was the custom of the time, young men from good families often became pages (or, in 21st-century terminology, interns), to serve in a nobleman's house in order to be educated in manners. Cherubino is receiving an education that is probably not the one his parents had in mind, for Cherubino is in love with love. He is caught by the Count flirting with Barbarina, the gardener's daughter. He flirts with Susanna in her room and has to hide quickly when the Count appears unexpectedly. Discovery nearly happens a third time when Cherubino is in the Countess' rooms declaring his love for her by way of a song, *"Voi che sapete."* In this arietta Cherubino describes his nascent feelings of love: "I have a feeling, full of desire, which now is pleasure, now torment. My spirit all ablaze, next moment I turn to ice." The Countess is sympathetic to his yearning but, in *The Marriage of Figaro*, does not encourage the boy. Cherubino is devastated when the Count assigns him a commission in the army and orders him to leave at once.

His very name a diminutive of the angelic cherubs of love, Cherubino disturbs the hearts and dreams of the women in the opera. Fluttering and winged, even Figaro refers to him as *"farfallone amoroso,"* ("amorous butterfly"). Kierkegaard, in his book, *Either/Or*, describes Cherubino in his three stages of love: the first stage suggested by the page in *Figaro*, the second by the simple, seeking Papageno in *The Magic Flute*, and the third by the libertine Don Giovanni. Kierkegaard says of Cherubino, "The sensuous awakens to a hushed tranquillity; not to joy and gladness, but to a deep melancholy. Desire is not yet awake, but only a gloomy foreboding." Cherubino's first intimations of love are described in Mozart's music as "quiet desire, quiet longing, and quiet ecstasy. Desire, in Cherubino, is only a presentiment for he only dreams of love."

The third couple in the opera are Marcellina and Bartolo, an unlikely pair. Marcellina appears near the start of the opera angrily complaining to Dr. Bartolo that she has rights. In her hand is a contract, a contract with Figaro, who had borrowed a sizeable sum of money from her and who, the contract states, must marry her if he does not repay the money. With Figaro's marriage to Susanna imminent, Marcellina is determined to see justice done and marry Figaro herself. Bartolo eagerly agrees to help her since he has his own axe to grind with Figaro, who was responsible for the Count's elopement and marriage to Rosina, the ward Bartolo planned to marry in *The Barber of Seville*. Marcellina's angry denouncement of Figaro fits nicely into the Count's plans. If Susanna agrees to his proposals, the Count will give her and Figaro a dowry that would pay off the debt to Marcellina. But if Susanna will not acquiesce, the Count will stop the marriage by withholding the dowry. As the Count gets increasingly angry at Susanna's refusals, he calls together a farcical court of law with Marcellina, Figaro, Don Curzio, a stuttering lawyer, and himself as judge.

Marcellina states her case. Don Curzio gives his opinion: "Pay up or marry her!" The Count is delighted. Figaro says he cannot marry without his parents' permission, for he is of noble birth. His parents, he says, abandoned him at birth, leaving only a birthmark on his arm as identification. Marcellina gasps as she recognizes the birthmark of the son she bore Dr. Bartolo. The infant had been stolen and had the same mark. "Raffaello!" she cries out. There follows one of the funniest scenes in opera, as the truth dawns that Figaro is indeed the son of Marcellina and Bartolo. Figaro is amazed — and relieved, for now he cannot marry Marcellina, who is his mother. Marcellina is ecstatic, Bartolo stunned, Don Curzio annoyed, and the Count furious at this new frustration. Susanna comes in at this moment, astonished to find Figaro in Marcellina's arms. The whole recognition scene is played again for her benefit. Bartolo, though not entirely happy at the ways things are working out, does the honorable thing and agrees to marry Marcellina; there will be a double wedding. The F-major sextet that happens at this point is thrilling, expressing simultaneously the differing thoughts and emotions of the six characters.

The "pay-up or marry" ruling may seem strange to us today, but there was precedent for it very close to home. When Mozart was a penniless musician, he stayed with the Weber family, a mother and four daughters. He spent so much time with Constanze that people began to talk — was Mozart going to marry her or not? If not, then Constanze was being compromised. The mother, eager to see her daughters wed, came up with a solution by asking Mozart to sign a document that said if he did not marry Constanze he would pay the family a large sum of money. When she heard of this Constanze tore up the document, and Mozart married her anyway.

The remaining characters, according to the operatic tradition of the time, each had to have at least one aria. Dr. Bartolo's aria comes in the first act, when he sings *"La vendetta,"* a tirade against Figaro, on whom he wants revenge. The arias of Marcellina and Basilio, the music master, occur in the last act, and both are usually cut, which is a pity. Marcellina's aria is a rebuttal to Figaro's criticism of women. She sings, "We, poor women, who so love these men, are treated by the traitors with constant perfidy." Marcellina has a major change of heart when she finds she is Figaro's mother, and when she learns that Bartolo will marry her after all. Now she takes Susanna's part and assures Figaro that Susanna can be trusted.

Basilio's aria is an odd little treatise that says it is dangerous to clash with "important people" because the lesser man cannot win. "Fate made me realize that shame, dangers, humiliation, and death can be avoided beneath an ass's skin" (i.e., if I stay in my place as a servant). After all that has gone before with Figaro and Susanna constantly challenging and outwitting the Count, Basilio's words are surprising.

The story of *The Marriage of Figaro* is complex, but accessible in performance. Moving away from the traditional long string of arias, Mozart has his characters interact with one another in duets and ensembles. The ensembles that end Acts II (a twenty-minute finale of three movements), and IV (sung by all eleven principals) are thrilling and exciting.

Humor was a great strength of Mozart's. In *Figaro* there are many *coups de théâtre,* or great surprises, that provoke laughter at the human foibles of characters in whom we all too often see ourselves. The hide-and-seek nonsense of the first act is broad comedy: Cherubino hides in Susanna's room as the Count enters, the Count hides (almost in the same place) as Basilio enters, and Cherubino finally is discovered. The closet scene is amusing when the audience is let in on the secret as to who is and who is not hiding in the closet. The recognition scene, in which Figaro finds out that Marcellina is his mother, is hilarious; this time the audience is as surprised as the characters on stage. There is more: the dressing-up of Cherubino, the drunken gardener and his broken flower pots, the stuttering lawyer. The final *coup de théâtre* is pure chaos, as everyone is confused as to who is meeting whom in which arbor in the garden.

But finally it all unravels and truth is revealed: the Count is caught making love to his own wife, believing her to be Susanna. This is the moment we all wait for, that transcendent moment when the Countess forgives her contrite husband. Her absolution ends all the misunderstandings in the shadowed garden; it is a blessing in music. Rosina rises above her personal pain and grief, forgiving herself, along with Figaro, whose intrigues and brief doubt of Susanna's faithfulness are forgiven; Cherubino, for his dalliances in his first hesitant steps on the path to love; and Marcellina and Bartolo, whose petty jealousies nearly destroyed the happiness of the onetime barber and his bride. Only Susanna comes through the crazy day with her spirit (and body) intact, eager for her wedding to Figaro, whom she truly loves. The Count, we sense, will sin again, but for this moment, this perfect moment, the forgiveness and compassion of the Countess, and Mozart, are enough.

International director Bruce Donnell stages this production first seen in Santa Fe in 2008, John Nelson conducts. Daniel Okulitch, last seen as The Last Savage is transformed into Count Almaviva, Susanna Phillips sings his Countess. American singer Lisette Oropesa makes a company debut as Susanna and Figaro is sung by Zachary Nelson.

♪

Characters

Count Almaviva	Baritone
Countess Almaviva	Soprano
Figaro, valet to the Count	Bass
Susanna, maid to the Countess	Soprano
Cherubino, page to the Count	Soprano
Dr. Bartolo	Bass
Marcellina, housekeeper	Soprano

Bibliography

Beaumarchais, Caron de. *The Barber of Seville and The Marriage of Figaro*. John Wood, trans. New York: Penguin, 1964.

Bolt, Rodney. *The Librettist of Venice*. Bloomsbury Publishing, New York, 2006.

Mersmann, Hans, ed. *Letters of Mozart*. Dorset Press, New York, 1986.

Levey, Michael. *The Life and Death of Mozart*. Stein & Day, New York, 1972.

Osborne, Charles. *The Complete Operas of Mozart*. Da Capo Press, New York, 1978.